Inside / Outside

Malcolm Grear

Inside / Outside

From

the Basics

to

the Practice

of

Design

VAN NOSTRAND REINHOLD
_____ New York

Van Nostrand Reinhold is an
I(T)P International Thomson Publishing company.
ITP logo is a trademark under license.

Van Nostrand Reinhold
115 Fifth Avenue
New York, New York 10003

International Thomson Publishing
Berkshire House, 168-173
High Holborn, London WC1V 7AA
England

Thomas Nelson Australia
102 Dodds Street
South Melbourne 3205
Victoria, Australia

Nelson Canada
1120 Birchmount Road
Scarborough, Ontario
M1K 5G4, Canada

International Thomson Publishing GmbH
Konigswinterer Str. 518
5300 Bonn 3
Germany

International Thomson Publishing Asia
38 Kim Tian Road, #0105
Kim Tian Plaza
Singapore 0316

International Thomson Publishing Japan
Kyowa Building, 3F
2-2-1 Hirakawacho
Chiyada-Ku, Tokyo 102
Japan

Design: Malcolm Grear
Printed in the United States of America
on Mohawk Poseidon Perfect White

16 15 14 13 12 11 10 9 8 7 6 5 4 3 2 1

Library of Congress Cataloging in Publication Data

Grear, Malcolm.
Inside / Outside: From the Basics to the Practice
of Design / Malcolm Grear
p. cm.
Includes index.
ISBN 0-442-01667-0
1. Graphic arts — Study and teaching.
2. Graphic arts — Practice.
1. Title.
NC1000.G74 1993   93-18988
741.6-DC20   CIP

Contents

9 **Introduction**
10 **Acknowledgments**
11 **Graphic Design**
15 **My Training**

17 **Student Assignments**

19 The Form of a Maple Leaf
20 **Letterform Studies**
20 Letters as Forms
25 The Form of a Letter
26 Free Form and Structure
28 Combining Free and Structured Forms
33 Letterform on 3/D Surface
34 2/D and 3/D Combinations
40 The Form of a Chair
42 2/D Chairform to a 3/D Object
43 Chairforms and Letterforms Combined
44 Field in Motion
46 Formal Qualities of a Letter
49 Form and Structure
66 Forms Progressing
78 A Structural Framework
80 Juxtaposing Images
82 Visual Connections
86 Overview
88 **Ten Steps**
88 Steps, Sequence, and Series
96 Function of a Handtool
104 Combining Visual Stories
106 Transforming a Letter
110 A Word's Meaning Visualized
113 Visual Comparisons
123 Variations on a Theme
124 Analyzing Form
127 One to Ten
129 Essence of an Object
135 Containers/Contents
136 Type and Image
141 **Letterforms and Typography**
143 Typographic Form
164 Symbols/Signs
171 Graphic Standards Manual
172 Design Application

177 **Professional Practice**
178 **From School to Studio**
179 **From Student to Professional**
181 **Design as a Business**

183 **Design Commissions**

184 Counterform/Form
190 Line, Weight, and Dimension
194 Visual Switch
197 Light and Tension
198 Interpretation
200 Dual Visual Meaning
204 Sun in Symbols
206 Expanded Meaning
209 Constantly Moving
210 Humor in Design
212 Crisis and Resolution
216 Manual of Graphic Standards
218 Non-Repetitive Identity
220 Welcome
223 Signs Without Words
226 Function Following Form
228 Time, Space, and Position
230 Scale Relationship
232 Light and Shadow
235 Signs
242 Balance
248 Black and White
252 Black and Gray Called Black and White
254 Layering
261 One of a Kind
262 Visual Sympathy
266 Sequencing, Relating, and Pacing
274 2/D Grid Structure
276 Horizontal and Vertical
278 Disguising the Grid
280 Exhibition Design
282 3/D Structure
284 Beyond Structure

287 **Doing This Book**
289 **A Way of Working**
290 **Learning to Listen**
291 **Other Lessons Learned**
293 **Joy**
295 **Coda**
297 **Index**

Introduction

"To distribute material things is to divide them.

To distribute spiritual things is to multiply them."

J O S E F   A L B E R S

I am with this book attempting to distribute what might loosely be considered "spiritual things"—the things I tried to teach students and the things they succeeded in teaching me during three decades at the Rhode Island School of Design (RISD).

The basic idea came from past students, now professional designers, who suggested that I document assignments I give my classes at RISD. The tables are turned. Students have given their teacher an assignment. I tackle it willingly because I presume to believe that the success my students have attained as designers is, to some extent, based on what and how they learned by doing exercises for me, and these exercises, which are the backbone of this book, might well be useful to others.

One theme I explore in these pages is the relationship between education and professional practice. I attempt this exploration because I am a professional designer who happens also to be teaching; I have experience in both realms and have learned useful things from each. It is my view that teachers of design should continue to practice in the professional arena. They need not, probably should not, teach what they do as professionals, but solving design problems in the "real" world of commerce prepares a teacher to stimulate students' intuition and imagination more vigorously than is possible if the teacher remains captured by the walls of academe.

I don't, indeed can't, teach students to be designers, but I can and do teach attitudes and strategies that help them become designers. My work outside the classroom informs my didactic methods and, I think, improves them.

I include in this book assignments that I give my classes and assignments that clients have given me and my colleagues at Malcolm Grear Designers; it is not a complete documentation of either area. My classes are only a modest part of a larger curriculum at RISD, and the examples included here are only part of the total I assign; likewise, examples derived from my studio represent a minor fraction of work done there.

I make no attempt to present a system of design. Even if I were to succeed at so grand a scheme, it would be fruitless. Those who adopted such a system might gain manipulative skill but would be ill-prepared to cope with ideas. And the expression of ideas is the origin of design—and its purpose.

In this quickly changing world it is now more important than ever that graphic designers be trained to solve problems in an open, responsive, and flexible manner. If students are placed in a mold, their work will soon become irrelevant.

In designing, in teaching, and in this book, I follow the principle of inside-out: from inner to outer form; from inside the studio or classroom to the world outside. The exercise of this principle prompts me to examine small, inner parts of an object, process, or idea in order to understand the whole. Most of my classroom assignments begin with fragments of things or ideas that develop into more comprehensive schemes, from the inside-out. It is a reductionist strategy, much used by scientists, much lamented by humanists. Don't get me wrong. The reductionist process is often necessary but never sufficient. There is no substitute for seeing the big picture, the entire system.

Kentucky Patchwork Quilt
circa 1940

Acknowledgments

I want to thank all of my students from the past thirty years; they have made this book possible—not only those whose work is shown, but each and every one of them. Their classroom contributions form an integral part of my development as a teacher and professional designer. Their work and spirit pervade the pages of this book and the days of my life.

I should like to give individual credit for each piece of student work shown, but these were classroom exercises and there is no longer any record of who did what. I take the liberty of showing these exercises out of context, outside the classroom circumstances in which they were devised, because I see them not as objects but as parts of an educational method, footprints on the path toward becoming a designer.

It is this path that I am attempting to reveal. I want to convey the dynamic act of invention, not just the results. I suppose what I really want to do is somehow to transmit to readers a sense of how one can release in oneself the controlled freedom so essential to the creation of effective design. The pleasure (and pain) is in the doing—as with the rest of life or, rather, the rest of *living*. Art is a verb; design is a verb. Objects result, of course. But, for the designer, the act of designing is the point; it is this action that must be studied and practiced and enjoyed for its own sake.

To

students

colleagues

my

family

and

my dear friend

Neil Patterson

who has

helped

me

with

my words

Graphic Design

"If you work intensely and slowly, things will happen that you would never imagine."

AARON SISKIND, 1990

The dictionary definition of graphic, "giving a clear and effective picture," reveals a key function of graphic design: to convey information. As with music, design can set a mood, generate tension, surprise, or calm; it can startle or seduce. But all of these emotional states, and many others, are for the designer a kind of information. Music in a movie tells you what to think or feel about what's going on. In a sense, design does the same thing—it tells you how to respond to the rest of the message embodied in the graphics. And, again, like music, or like smell, the visual signals shoot straight to the emotions. That is the power of graphics. Language, although immensely powerful, seems less immediate, less swiftly channeled into the emotional regions of our minds.

Graphic design is not an independent, private art, such as most painting, sculpture, or music, although it draws upon these disciplines; it is a public enterprise, devising ways to communicate information through form, color, texture, and the other visual signals.

"Professional" design can be said to have started in earnest in the United States in the 1930s, although designing is an activity as ancient as the human species, and it came more clearly into focus in the 1950s, locating itself between the fine arts and advertising art. The first generation of graphic designers wanted to separate themselves from advertising, which some saw, rather preciously, as the sleazy side of graphic communication since they considered it tainted by commercial intentions.

This disdain for, and suspicion of, commerce was in part a response to the perceived need for more objective, more ethically responsible graphic communication.

These pioneers of graphic design wished to see themselves as more socially responsible than their cohorts in the world of "commercial advertising art." They wanted to use images and type, color and form, and other design elements to convey information vividly but honestly instead of dressing up hard-sell copy to seduce buyers. Despite these efforts at separation, the distinction between graphic design and commercial art is often blurred since both serve the needs of business.

Graphic design at its best attempts to deliver direct visual communications while most "commercial art" is meant to entice. But enticement is a form of communication, too, and often a worthy one. Nor can it be said that all advertising is without integrity nor that those inventing it have no concern for truth and aesthetics. It is simply that those involved in advertising as a profession need not focus on such matters. Their purpose, quite sensibly, is to sell.

A comparable analogy can be made between the interior architect and interior decorator. The architect is, for the most part, concerned with form and function; the decorator is usually concerned with embellishment, although function is often part of the decorator's purpose, and form, for its own sake, has deep and rightly honored traditions in architecture. As the old saying goes: "Comparisons are odious." These distinctions are frequently gratuitous and ill-conceived.

As a kid growing up in Kentucky, I thought art was the label on a Cloverene salve tin or a magazine cover by Norman Rockwell. I had no idea about design, much less graphic design. Yet, life (and my nature?) led me into this field; I became, unavoidably, a graphic designer and have never wished to be anything else.

Early in my career I remember watching a group of business people, thinking how unfortunate they were because they didn't have a profession that they cared about as much as I cared about mine. This, of course, was ridiculous. They may have been thinking the same thing about me, whatever they imagined my work to be. This happened thirty-one years ago and I still have the same passion for design. I want everyone to understand what it is all about.

I learned much from my father, a first-class carpenter and cabinetmaker. He taught me to take care in what I do—the results, he said, would be compensation enough. He used to tell me that his tables were made for those who look underneath to see how they are constructed. He didn't care what I became: "Just like what you do, and do it well."

I can still see my father standing by the bus as I board to leave for the Navy. I am sitting in the bus, next to an open window; he looks up at me and says, "Be a man." By this I know he means: Be honest and do good things. This smacks of Hollywood sentimentality, but it rang true to me; still does.

This book tries to show that view of work, the view I learned from my father. If a carpenter or waitress can't read this book and make sense of it, then it's no good. The subject should be accessible to anyone who has the time to look—and, even better, the time to do.

If we were dealing with science, let's say physics, then this book would be about *doing* physics: it is a lab course, not theory. Design is about doing; it is an act, a process.

If you track a design project from beginning to end, it is not so different from work in other professions, say that of a writer, doctor, or lawyer. You stay with the project until you get it right. You include whomever and whatever may be needed to accomplish the goal.

The designer may serve as choreographer, but most jobs depend on many dancers to bring an idea to fruition. A designer with too much ego may forget that his work involves many people, including the client. Those involved may be writers, photographers, illustrators, editors, architects, engineers, computer specialists, publishers, typesetters, printers—a host of people who hold the job together and make it work. If communication among collaborators breaks down, if vanity intrudes, the project suffers. A designer must welcome others into the effort; it is a social transaction.

This book is an example. Many people, beginning with my students at the Rhode Island School of Design and my colleagues at Malcolm Grear Designers, have helped to make it happen. The students produced the exercises reprinted here; my co-workers influenced content and organization.

It could not have been possible without the assistance of many knowledgeable and generous people. A special note of gratitude is due Patricia Appleton for her great skill and her sensitivity and devotion to all aspects of this publication; Martha Schneider for editorial suggestions and her patience in keeping the manuscript straight through many changes. Pat and Martha are colleagues at Malcolm Grear Designers.

Leah Grear, an artist and my daughter, picked up my thumbnail sketches and laid out nearly every page.

Another strong influence was Neil Patterson, my close friend and a connoisseur of words and images. Neil is a publisher of scientific books. He taught me stuff about sentences and helped in other ways.

Some of the reasons for attempting this project are negative. There is, to my mind, more than enough talk about graphics these days, way too much theory. This is an applied field, like engineering or clinical medicine. I am convinced that students learn by doing, by fiddling, and by practicing. So this book is full of exercises. Theory, which is thin soup in the art world, is seldom mentioned. My intention—one that I now fear I have failed to follow rigorously enough—is to avoid the jargon of graphic design and art criticism.

Our world is overstocked with images—mostly clutter—from computer monitors, movie and television screens, product packaging, billboards, magazines, and other print media. We are bombarded by a numbing array of visual "information." There is little chance of slowing down this high-speed, high-tech culture. We have to adapt. One adaptation that will reduce confusion and offer some solace is improved graphic design.

We are a visual species. Most of us are strongly affected by the signals that reach our brain through our eyes. We seem able to tolerate an astonishing diversity of "visual noise" generated by urban crowding and decay; but we are soothed by the look of trees and fields, the ocean, open sky, art and architecture, and other signs of visual grace—a handsome book, a piece of cloth, any object, place, or creature that we find attractive.

It is for this reason that graphic design has an increasingly significant role to play: Along with architecture, resource management, and environmental planning, it helps to shape much of our world and will shape more of it in times to come. So it matters that designers of products, and designers of messages that promote those products, do their work with a sense of responsibility. We serve a human need for clear, engaging forms of visual communication. This need is more profound and pervasive than we might think. It is not for nothing that we—and all cultures—spend so much time and substance arranging environments to satisfy this need. Not for nothing, too, that we pay so steep a price in stress related ailments when we neglect the need for visual harmony.

Teaching students how to solve a particular design problem is sometimes appropriate, but it is not the main purpose of a course such as mine. The take-home lesson for the student is the process by which a solution is achieved. Given that there are usually many acceptable solutions to any problem in design, to concentrate on results rather than process is to shortchange students and inhibit their development.

One must see problems in context. A designer needs to take account of the nature and needs of the people who are to use the design. The users are not just those who hire the designer; users also include the "consumers" of the design. If this entire set of circumstances, the state of the total system, remains unexamined, the designer is in danger of plugging in preconceived "solutions" without taking full account of the problem at hand. The designer who solves a problem within its context will not have to worry about doing something original. The outcome will be new because the problem was solved in accord with its context. Each context is unique; a successful solution will likewise be unique.

I like a lot the adage that for every problem there is a solution that is simple, obvious, and wrong. A problem worthy of the name is seldom accessible to sudden and simple solution. It may appear that way at times but usually because the solver, even unconsciously, has been steeped in the problem and its various ramifications and thus is able to experience revelation, sudden insight, as though it sprang full-blown from a brilliant mind. It is best to take it that problem solving is hard work. You might as well enjoy it.

As with clinicians, designers are in the problem solving business. So teachers help students most by gearing design education to problem solving. However, students should not be expected to—although they sometimes can—solve large, complicated design problems, the sort that takes years of education and experience to solve. I give them basic problems that they can see in full complexity.

A good number of the following pages are filled with students' work that illustrates this approach to design education. I pose basic problems and encourage the students to think about them holistically and then to work through a series of design progressions. The students learn ways of approaching problems; they learn some fundamental principles; and they become better and better equipped to solve ornate problems under elaborate constraints. Constraint, of course, is the name of the game. Problems confronted by professional designers are defined by the purpose a design must serve and the constraints imposed by unavoidable circumstances. Such constraints can involve time, money, materials, dimensions, audience, media, and a host of other factors.

It is my view that practicing designers, those who have a professional practice beyond their academic teaching responsibilities, will be likely to teach effectively following this problem-solving strategy. It is like the case method now used at graduate schools of business and, increasingly, at medical schools. Experience in the "real world" is essential background for this kind of teaching. Through professional practice the educator keeps abreast of current needs and is tested against others in the field. But let me repeat a caution: The designer, when teaching, must not simply pass on methods to students. The central task is to teach principles that students can apply over the long haul as they develop through professional work in the world beyond school.

Malcolm Grear
The Furrow 1951
Made from a steel plow point.

My Training

The ancient Greeks used to say that "Character is fate." Where does character come from? From the genes, to some extent, but also, surely, from "upbringing."

I am certain that my early years have a great deal to do with my viewpoint. I was born and spent my beginning years in rural Kentucky and reached my eleventh year before Rural Electric Association first installed electricity. Little was wasted in that time and place. Livestock feed bags became dresses that later became pieces of patchwork quilts. Our playthings were homemade; wooden thread spools served as wheels for toy trucks; logs were sawed to make larger wheels for the wagons we rode down hills. Whistles were formed from poplar bark or watermelon vine. These frugal devices prevail even today in the Kentucky countryside. Scraps of clothing still find their way into quilts and Clorox bottles are turned into windmills or birdhouses. As with farming people everywhere, we learned to make the most of what comes to hand.

After high school I opened a sign shop, which I operated for a year before joining the Navy. In the service, I was trained as an aviation metalsmith and became a welder of considerable skill. Four years later, to my surprise, I was accepted at the nearby Art Academy of Cincinnati on the basis of this metalsmithing experience. I served as a teaching assistant in the metal shop, where I produced several pieces of sculpture. This experience helped me see beyond two dimensions and broadened my sense of materials; it also gave me my first clear understanding of design as a pervasive force in nature and human action.

Each day began and ended with compulsory sketch class. Mornings were devoted to drawing, painting, printmaking or metal or woodworking. Afternoons were devoted to one's major. A visionary art history teacher made me aware of Lautrec, Miro, Kurt Schwitters, Matisse, and Man Ray, artists who also designed books and posters. Their work influenced my choosing design as a major. I learned early to avoid thinking that each visual art has an exclusive language. Visual dialect and idiom may vary, materials may vary, but there is unity across diverse kinds of art. My teachers introduced me to the work of the great photographers, and they have had an enduring effect on my own work. Man Ray's mysterious images, as well as his photograms, first persuaded me to see photography as an art form. Aaron Siskind's photographs compelled me to consider form and counterform in composition. Aaron is the one who did the most, in those years, to disabuse me of the notion that photography is largely technique. The critic Elaine de Kooning sensibly says that Siskind's work is "as highly personal as any painter could invent." Harry Callahan's split seconds in time and space also played a vivid role in my growing awareness of the power of photographic art, a power further revealed to me in those years by the works of Edward Steichen, Henri Cartier Bresson, Walker Evans, Stieglitz, and Herbert Matter. All of these photographers, and many others since, have influenced my work by teaching me to see.

I count myself fortunate to have been educated by members of the first generation of graphic designers in this country, sculptors, painters, and printmakers who were also designers and teachers. They taught at the Academy but took design commissions, never confusing the two levels of practice; they maintained integrity at both levels.

The Art Academy of Cincinnati attracted distinguished visiting critics, among them Jacques Lipchitz and Buchminster Fuller. The teaching itself was somewhat influenced by Josef Albers, for he had been a visiting professor before I entered.

I learned during this period that education engages emotion as well as reason. Reason alone is never enough, in art or science or any other human endeavor.

When I graduated, my teachers thought I was a sculptor, I thought they thought I was a photographer, but I knew I wanted to be a graphic designer.

Louise Nevelson said, "I feel like an artist—you feel it—just like you feel you are a singer if you have a voice. I have that blessing and there has never been a time that I questioned or doubted it. I have always wanted to show the world that art is everywhere except it has to pass through a creative mind." I feel that way about graphic design.

Malcolm Grear
From the Ashes 1960
Made from cast iron ash shakers
out of a coal furnace.

Malcolm Grear
Void 1957
Made from steel sewer pipes.

Student Assignments

The Form of a Maple Leaf

On the first day in class I try to give students a sense of what my course is all about. After some casual conversation, I assign a five-minute exercise: I ask how many of them are from New England. This leads to talk about the weather, fall colors, trees, and leaves. I ask if they know what a maple leaf looks like. They say, "Yes." I ask them to draw one in five minutes or less. Then I ask them to pass these drawings around so that each student sees all the sketches. If a classmate thinks a drawing is an accurate representation of a maple leaf, it gets a plus, if not, it gets a zero. With rare exceptions, each drawing ends up with abundant zeros and a few pluses.

I have kept many of these sketches over the years. They make me smile when I remember how confident the students were when picking up their pencils and how this confidence turned to frustration when they began to draw.

I say, "What's up? You tell me you know what a maple leaf looks like but most of these drawings are plastered with zeros." They then realize that they recognize a maple leaf, can easily distinguish it from other kinds of leaves, but can't draw one because they have never examined and considered its inner form.

This exercise establishes a principle that pervades my course: There is no substitute for knowledge about the object or process one is attempting to convey through graphic design. If leaves are a factor in your work, study leaves.

Letterform Studies

Those who know the work of photographer Aaron Siskind and designer Norman Ives will notice their influence on my teaching. It is particularly evident in the first three letterform exercises I assign: Siskind's fragmenting of images and Ives' fragmenting of letterforms.

One of my early pleasures at the Rhode Island School of Design was helping to persuade Norman Ives to teach there in 1961 through 1963 and, again, in 1965 through 1968. We remained close friends until his death in 1978. Ives and I taught the same courses, and so began the development of our assignments; they are no longer the same as they were at the outset—they evolve in response to experience in the classroom—but their point of origin is clear.

As for dear Aaron Siskind, he and I continued our friendship until his death in 1991, and his photographs continue to have fresh life for me. Among many other things, Siskind helps me see in new ways, to reverse the normal way of looking at things—in his work, negative space becomes positive form. I have on my living room wall a large Siskind photograph of a stone fence, close up; the spaces around the stones are dominant forms in their own right. The power of this space is astonishing. Siskind saw it and makes us see it. It's a lesson I never forget.

Letters as Forms

Beginning students of graphic design are often haunted by the prospect of dealing throughout their careers with an essential, mundane, but daunting tool of their trade—the letterform, in all its subtle ramifications. When asked to describe the typefaces prevalent in their textbooks in earlier school years, few, if any, will remember anything about them. While this is an understandable, even necessary, state of affairs for most of us—we would overburden our senses if we took notice of every detail of all signals that swarm to our eyes—it is not acceptable for a graphic designer.

Each of us is affected in slight, and sometimes significant, ways by the forms of typefaces and by the spaces on which they are placed, but only a trained eye is likely to discern nuances of shape, pattern, and texture that engender those responses. The look of the page you are reading now, for example, is probably influencing your mood in a manner different from the mood prompted by the novel, newspaper, or annual report you were reading recently—and this response is less dependent on content and more on form than you may realize. The following assignment is intended to begin training the eye, to instill a sensitivity to, and control over, the multifarious world of letterforms.

For this assignment, I ask students to create with letterforms a composition that expresses a mood, thought, or action. I usually specify a square format because it doesn't impose direction. With a square, there is no insistence on horizontal or vertical array. A final constraint: These compositions depend on the form of letters, not their symbolic qualities. No single letters should stand out. We are not going to "read" the results in the ordinary meaning of that term. We are going to watch the behavior of the visual space shaped by interplay of form and counterform.

Since I want students to begin forming their own ideas about typefaces, they must examine newspapers and magazines and gather their letters from these sources. If the type is in color, printed on newsprint, or printed on coated paper, they have to take these aspects into account when constructing their work.

Through this exercise students become more familiar with various letterforms and begin to understand that each type-face has its own personality. You can cut a letter into sections, but it is curiously difficult to obliterate its letterform identity as long as you retain an outside edge.

And through this exercise I get to know the students better and begin to understand their personalities. For example, a student who likes to work with things that are fussy or intricate will choose smaller letterforms. One student's project was a quarter of an inch thick by the time he had finished it. He started with a Bristol board base and used literally thousands of small letterforms to construct his piece. A student in the same class worked with only five letterforms. Same assignment, different worker, sharply different result. Despite the force of tradition, art diversifies—an endlessly evolving process, an infinite delight.

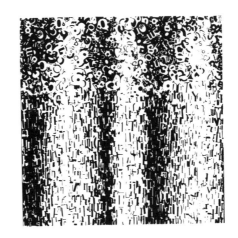

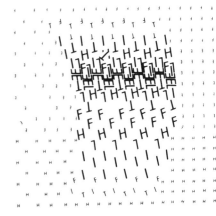

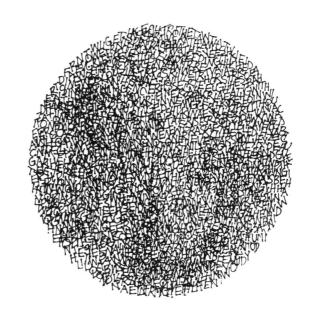

The Form of a Letter

The next exercise, which continues consideration of the letter as form, involves removing as much of the letter as possible while leaving enough to allow its identification. This assignment brings into focus those qualities of a letter that make it different from others. It is not important to end up with a letterform that is immediately identifiable; it is enough to insure that, after a process of elimination, the remaining form could not be derived from any other letter. The final composition should also have roughly equal amounts of black and white, figure and ground, form and counterform. The letter can be altered as long as its integrity remains intact. Lively design often breaks rules.

Students begin this exercise by working with a printed black letter on a white surface, cutting away pieces of the letter, enlarging the remaining form, and, perhaps, redrawing it. Final dimensions are usually in the range of a 19″ × 19″ square, executed in gouache, black on a painted white surface.

The next step is to reverse the composition—placing white on a black surface. Students are usually startled to discover that a white image on a black field appears larger than black on white. Thus the form must be redrawn to make black and white appear equal. Equal, of course, is seldom strictly equal when dealing with vision; dimensional equality may need adjustment to achieve visual equality.

As the design evolves, letter parts give way to the space around them or, sometimes, the space gives way to the parts. In either case, the form of an object is not more important than the form of the space surrounding it. The Yin Yang symbol embodies this idea: All things exist in interaction with other things. In music, are the separations between notes less important than the notes themselves? Isn't it the interlude, the quiet tension, between bursts of action in baseball that makes the game so intriguing?

Incidentally, another value of this exercise is the student's improved sense of how to alter a line in a way that encourages the viewer to imagine its continuation.

The letter fragment is easily recognizable when a complete letter is included in the composition.

I ask the students to make photocopies of the work they produced for the preceding assignments—black on white and white on black—and then, in one composition, to combine these photocopies as a free form and, in another, to build a structured form (grid), creating an arrangement not just by repeating a pattern (parquet) but by manipulating form and counterform, figure and ground. Once they assemble these compositions I ask them to rearrange the relationship between form and counterform in both versions. Often I ask them to cut each composition diagonally in both directions and rearrange the components until they achieve an array of figure/ground relationships where neither figure nor ground is dominant and the whole set of forms is in balance.

My intention here is not to teach balance for its own sake. Balance has no special virtue in graphic design; indeed, much good design relies on dissonance and imbalance among forms, colors, and textures. Rather, I attempt with these assignments to engender in the student, from the inside out, a familiarity with letterforms and the spaces created by their juxtaposition. By taking a letter apart and manipulating its fragments—not at random but with goals in mind, in this case balance between figure and ground—the student gains an intimate sense of that letter in particular and, with further practice, of letters in general, and begins to develop intuition about letterspacing, type design, and other aspects of typography. This dismantling and rearranging of letterforms is done in a spirit of experimentation, a kind of play. I want students to experience the tension between freedom and constraint. And I very much want them not to depend on rules—at least, not solely on rules—because there are no reliable rules that lead to successful letterspacing or any other element of design. You can't learn physics or other sciences without doing experiments. The same holds for graphic design. Theory is nice; experiment is necessary.

A sixteen unit structure that allows for constancy and change.

The single unit.

These exercises are also meant to foster an understanding of letterforms as works of art, however precious that may sound. Letters are signals, to be sure; their function is to convey meaning. But they are more than little bits of messages. Their architecture can be examined and appreciated without reference to meaning, much the way one takes pleasure in a bridge or building without being solely preoccupied with function. Witness our delight in Chinese or Arabic letters even when their meaning remains mysterious.

Furthermore, familiarity with the structure of a typeface allows use of its attributes to convey information beyond the literal content of words. A passage set in a serif typeface is likely to induce in a reader's mind a somewhat different mood than would the same passage set in a sans serif face. Typefaces do have "personalities," individual characteristics that, taken together, convey subtleties not inherent in the language itself. There is nothing strange in this. Different colors suggest different moods. So do different notes on the musical scale. The medium is unavoidably part of the message. These experiments with letters, in free and structured contexts, begin the student's education in the diversity and power of letterforms.

Free form composition.

Combining Free and Structured Forms

In this series of letterform studies, each assignment includes the previous one. Patterns intensify as images increase in complexity.

The process begins with investigation of the unique qualities of a single letter. By examining the form of that letter, all twenty-five others in the alphabet have to be considered and their individual differences recognized.

The next composition gives equal emphasis to the definitive form of the letter and the space around it.

Next we combine an even number of reductions (let's say sixteen) of the prior assignment, organized to form a larger composition. At this point, attention shifts from the relationship between form and its surrounding space to the formation of equal amounts of black and white, each giving way to the other. In other words, counterform in the first composition may now appear as form; prior form may become counterform.

Two compositions have been created: One based on a simple grid, the other free form; both reveal the power of space within compositions.

The grid is an organizing structure, not a procrustean bed; it need not be followed slavishly, but it should strongly influence arrangements.

Then the free and structured forms must be combined in a single composition that retains the aesthetics of both; each should be present in equal amounts, like threads in a fabric.

This layering of visual information gives a fleeting illusion of color—even though the image is black and white—and, quite often, the illusion of transparency, of seeing through the image. The structured design combined with the free form causes a visual event not evident before.

Single unit.

Free form.

Structured form.

A combination of free and structured form.

Single unit.

Combinations.

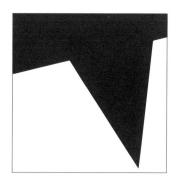

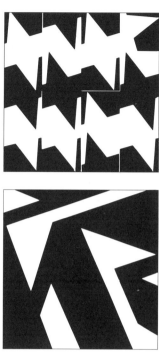

This set of assignments does not comprise a precise method for solving design problems; it flies in the face of the time-honored and worthy "form-follows-function" philosophy of design. But by weaving together free and structured forms, the student is developing skills that will help in solving design problems where form does follow function. This strategy can be applied to any design situation, two-dimensional or three-dimensional, to drawings, photographs, typography, books, posters, exhibits and so on. Again, it is the process that matters; the product will vary with circumstance.

Letterform on 3/D Surface

We now set the letterform on a cube and examine two-dimensional space applied to a three-dimensional surface.

Amounts of black and white change as the forms move around edges and corners of the cube. Once again adjustments must be made to compensate for the illusion of visual equality and to blend the forms.

While spinning the cube from diagonal points, black and white must occur in equal amount, giving the cube a grey haze when it is spinning, neither black nor white predominating.

33

In the next phase of the letterform exercise, we combine the image of the cube with the two-dimensional composition derived from the preceding exercise in order to create an illusion of three dimensions. Once again, neither part of the composition should be allowed to dominate.

First we take photographs of the cube from various angles and select from these the desired viewpoint. Then we do a drawing of the photograph, converting the cube to a two-dimensional image, which we combine with the composition produced for the previous assignment.

This letterform assignment, in all of its phases, turns out to be a series of combinations and interpretations; it began with a letterform study in two dimensions; this was converted into a three-dimensional study that was reconverted into two-dimensional form and combined with a previous two-dimensional composition to create the illusion of three dimensions.

The result of a series of combinations.

A progression of combinations from a 2/D
unit to a 3/D illusion.

Lines may be drawn into the composition
to emphasize the structure.

A collaborative effort among classmates.

If time allows, we may construct a class banner or mural.

Two studies of color: The students do two studies, one showing equal value of color intensity and one showing contrast. Adjustments are needed to make the images read properly.

Next, they combine parts in collaboration with their classmates.

At this point they begin to see that, when combined, the colors do not appear equal in amounts. When black is against black or white against white, the picture changes.

We extend the letterform assignment by examining the form of a chair.

I ask each student to delineate the unique qualities of one kind of chair and how it differs from others. These attributes must be expressed graphically, using a minimum amount of the chair form in a composition of equal amounts of black and white. I show pictures of classic chairs and ask each student to choose one of these or any other chair with which they would like to work.

Only a small percentage of the students are aware of the chairs by style, such as DeStijl, Barcelona, Eames Molded Plywood, Butterfly, Aalto, Corbu, and so on. They have seen most of the chairs before but never attached importance to their designers. Not a bad thing at this stage. This is a course in design, not history.

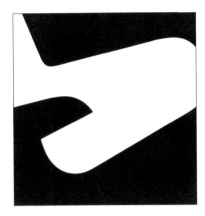

2/D Chairform to a 3/D Object

The two-dimensional exercise is once again applied to a cube structure. We use a hollow cube with half of each face removed, exposing twelve surfaces seen inside and through the cube; this structure reveals new interactions between form and counterform.

Placing images on panels and then juxtaposing them yields diverse relationships among forms. The form and counterform (black and white) allow a great variety of combinations. When the cube is rotated on its diagonal axis, the images should blend.

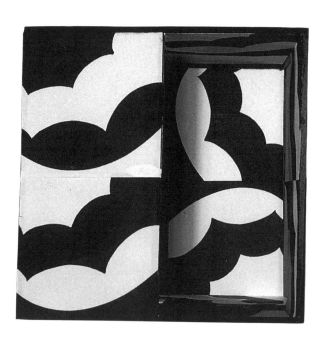

Actual and illusory visual connections.

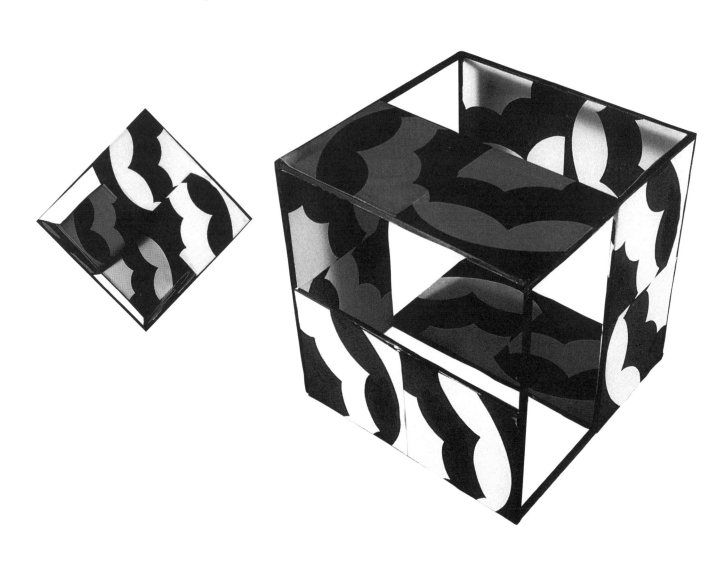

Chairforms and Letterforms Combined

Here the problem is to combine with the earlier letterform study a drawing of the chairform that has been applied to a three-dimensional surface, the cube.

The assignment introduces to beginning students the idea of combining into a single composition two types of visual information, the chair and the letter.

Field in Motion

In this assignment colored lines create a field that appears to be moving.

The lines are cut or torn from colored paper and placed on a 16″ square background.

Each line should be approximately 1/4″ wide by 3″ long and placed approximately 1/4″ from another line. I use the word "approximately" because, in this case, I want the students to visualize measurements rather than rely on rulers.

After completing this composition, students are asked to explain why the field appears to be oscillating.

Next, using a minimum number of lines of type placed on another board the same size as the one used for the array of colored lines, a composition is created that reflects the dynamics of the field of colored lines.

A typographic composition responding to adjacent visual field.

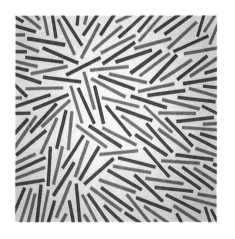

Formal Qualities of a Letter

In contrast to previous assignments, the purpose of this project is to look at the letter as a complete unit. Each letter must be completely defined and should not overlay another letter.

By using three or more of the same letter in the same size, a particular aspect of its form must be emphasized; each must appear as an integral part of the composition, which is placed on the square page with enough space around the unit so that it stands as a symbol.

Questions arise: At what point does an image have enough power to be symbolic? When does it have enough room to stand alone? When does it begin to take over the background? When does the whole structure fail to cohere? When does it become boring or "obvious?" How many letters become too many? In other words, when does the composition function as an effective symbol?

Duplication—This is unsuccessful because the L's appear as two pairs.

This arrangement fails because there are too many M's, creating a pattern.

WMW

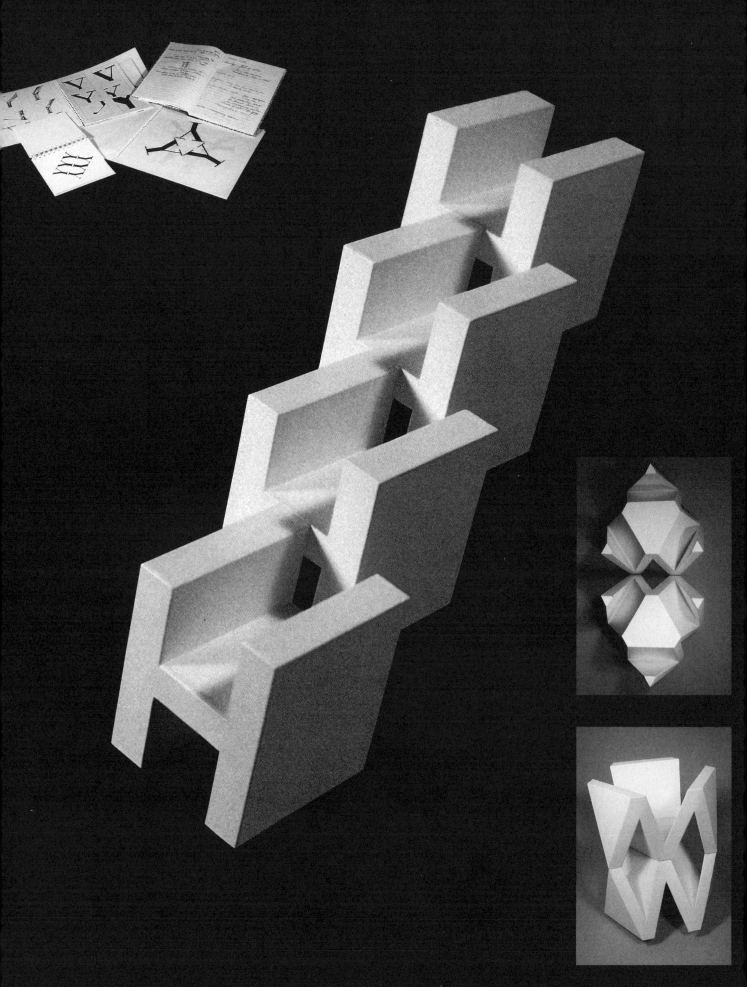

48

Form and Structure

This assignment begins with the selection of one of the studies from the earlier project, "Formal Qualities of a Letter."

The two-dimensional letter study is translated into a three-dimensional form. The 3/D structure shows the interrelating parts and "personality" of the study—the design subtleties—as revealed through close examination. The overall shape is not the issue.

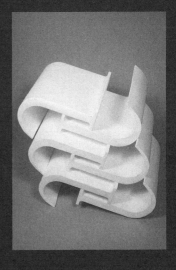

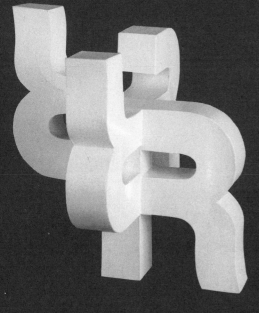

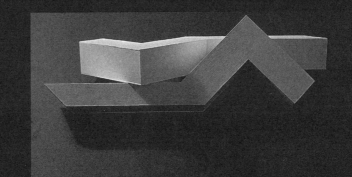

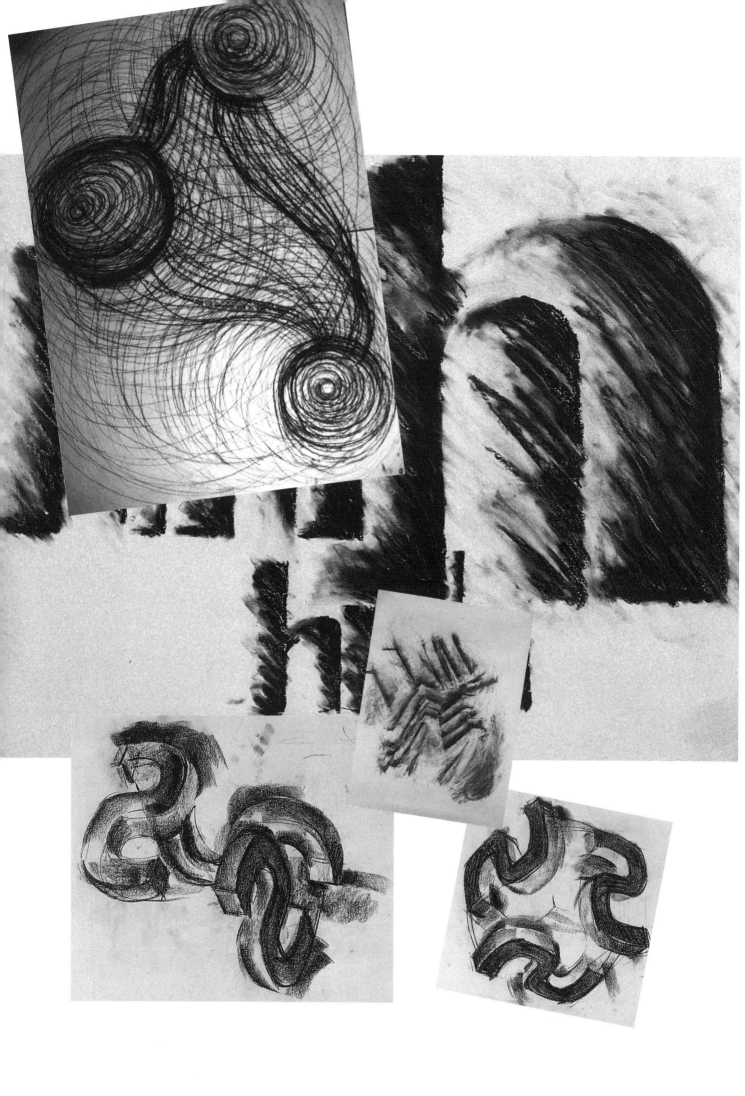

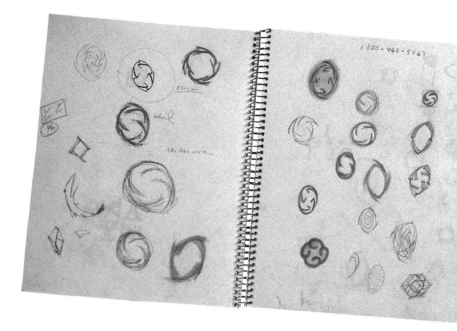

Once the construction has been built, students must "interpret" it through a series of drawings, emphasizing visual action: light, shadow, counterform, planes, and movement.

Once again, questions arise: What kind of visual glue is binding the 3/D composition together? Does the composition appear open or closed? Active or passive? What is more dominant, the counterform surrounding the letters or the letters themselves?

I try to get the students away from their desks at this point by encouraging them to make large drawings, at least 30″ to 40″ in one of the dimensions.

In the beginning, most feel insecure about their drawing skills and don't appreciate how much free-hand drawing improves visualization. They are wedded to the T-square and triangle or the computer, and they think all of their work should fit into their portfolios. Some seem to believe that anyone who draws, seriously, must have a "Fine Arts License." Many start out drawing with a tight, white-knuckled style, almost pushing the pencil through the paper.

They need encouragement and guidance during this phase: "Relax, trust your intuition; take more care, don't just rely on intuition; use a wide brush; try mixed media; move in closer; stand farther back."

Eventually, beautiful drawings begin to emerge; you can feel energy emanating from the class as the students close in on their work and discover that they are achieving more than they ever thought possible.

The visual solution includes drawings, photographs, words, and letterforms.

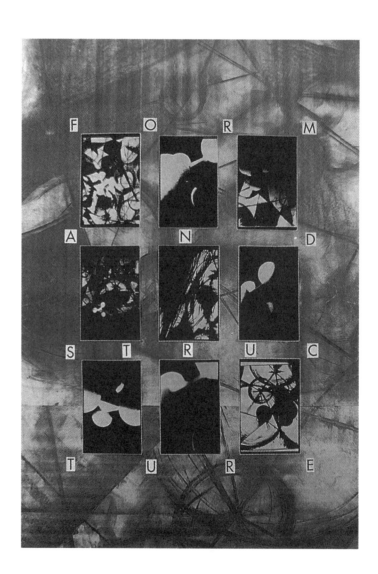

Structure

form=structure

The drawing study is followed by a photographic analysis of the three-dimensional form. You see things differently through the camera than you do when drawing. Of course, when you draw you can interpret, enhance, and exaggerate meaning in ways not possible with the camera.

sphere

plane

futu

geometry

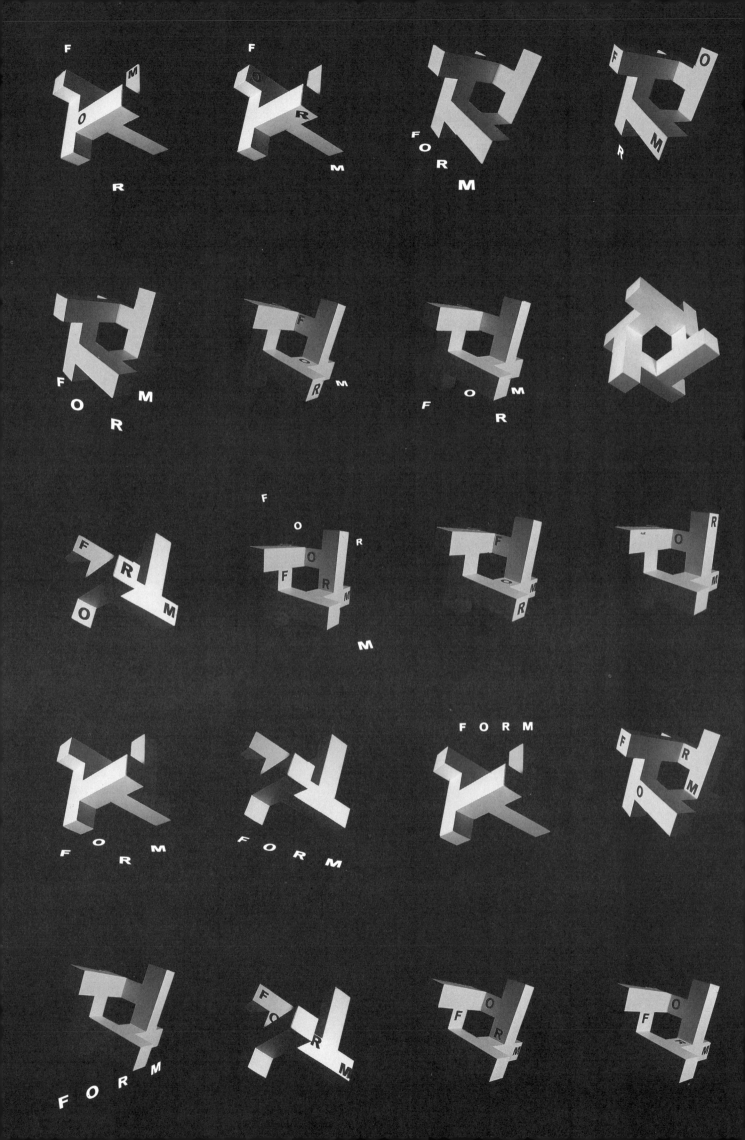

Next, the students must include a word or words with the constructed form and photograph the whole composition. The idea here is that the words must add a new dimension. As you can see from examples, sometimes the word only duplicates or emphasizes what is already there, but doesn't add much.

Now it is time to select from the studies those elements that can, by drawing or photography, be incorporated into a poster.

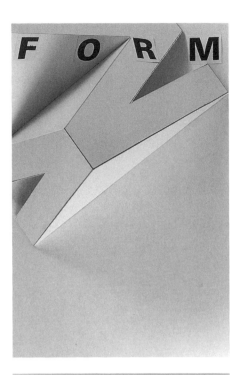

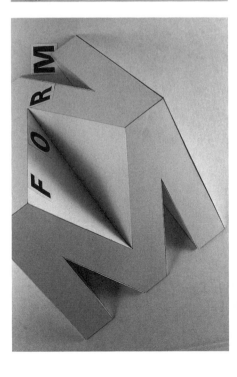

If the words don't make the poster stronger, the typography is at fault— either the wrong face is being used or size or placement is ill chosen.

If the image does not make the typography stronger, it may be the wrong image. Each of these elements, type and image, should reinforce the other.

If the words don't make the poster stronger, the typography is at fault— either the wrong face is being used or size or placement is ill chosen.

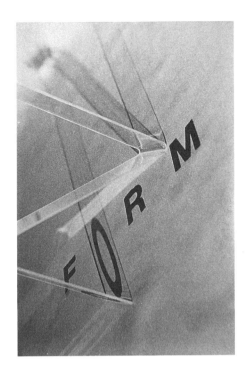

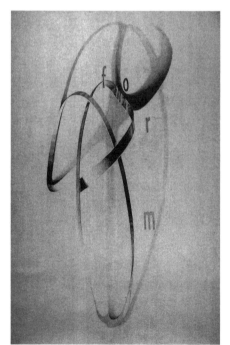

Topics for this assignment may change from year to year, but procedures remain fundamentally the same.

In this instance we translated a two-dimensional composition into a book with three-dimensional moveable parts. The three-dimensional pages were rendered in the form of large drawings and photographs, which were then recombined to make a two-dimensional book that includes words.

Some of the shapes are static while others have springs behind them. As you open the book, some of the shapes pop up and dance or quiver, contrasting with the stationary shapes, causing a flux of light, color, and shadow.

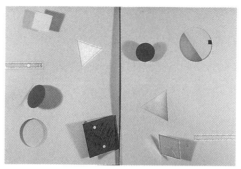

Forms Progressing

At this point, we move away from letterforms, but we don't abandon them. The students design a progression of pages in book form, using an accordion fold. They begin with a body of type or simple textures of type, such as the one illustrated at the bottom of the page. The design includes type and photographic images. The type and images should flow in a rhythmic progression, offering surprises as the pages are turned.

The accordion fold is used only to check the progression. It makes refinement and readjustment easy by allowing full view of the book at one time.

There are, of course, many ways to design the visual rhythm of a book.

One way is a smooth progression, a straight path, a "swoooosh" with no diversions.

An exciting progression can also be achieved by sharp contrasts within single pages, from page to page, or from double-page spread to double-page spread. Each new step can be a visual explosion, a sequence of surprises.

A simple way to advance from the block of type into the photographic forms is to use a series of even-step magnifications, moving in closer to the type. Photograph a section and enlarge it to full-page size. Photograph a section of the section and once again enlarge. Follow this process until you have moved in so close that only the form of a letter is seen, much like the bleed-off assignment (see page 24), where we concentrated on letters as forms. This enlarged letterform bridges the gap between letterforms and photographic forms.

The present assignment can be related to those maple leaf drawings produced in the first class. If we are some distance from a pile of leaves, we might vaguely see their shapes. If we move in closer, we see individual forms. If we pick up a leaf, we see its shape quite sharply. If we look even closer, we see its inner form. In like manner we are in this assignment examining the inner forms of photographs.

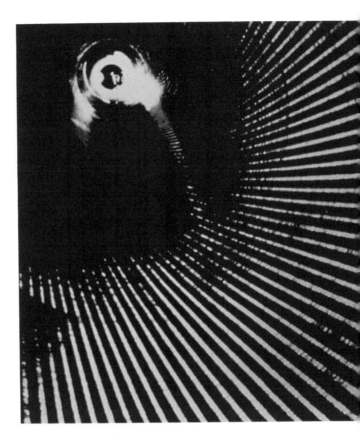

ONCE having traversed the threshold, the ... Road of Trials ...
ream landscape of curiously fluid, ambiguous ... 'am landscape ... landl la
ust survive a succession of trials. This is a favo ... st survive a survive al la
yth-adventure. It has produced a world literatu ... h-adventure ... survive
s and ordeals. The hero is covertly aided by ... and ordeal adven
re his entrance into this region. Or it may b ...
vers for the first time that there is a benign
e supporting him in his superhuman passage.
e of the best known and most charming exa
ult tasks" motif is that of Psyche's quest for h
Here all the principal roles are revers
ying to win his brid ...

The students are advised that the relationship between type and photographs in their books should not be based only on pattern. The progression must grow from the texture of a body of type to the inner forms of photographs. Do not see the photographs merely as rectangular pictures; instead be concerned with the qualities of form within the images. In other words, do not look at the photographs for their literal meaning. We may even turn the images upside down or move them around the edges of pages.

This exercise is designed to reveal photographic forms, not to display pictures; the end result is not meant to be a book of photographs.

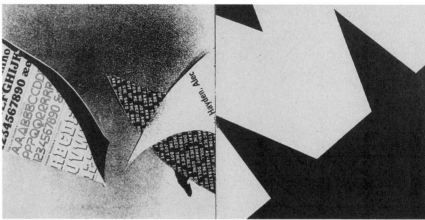

We are intending to enhance awareness of the dynamics of form and counterform within photographs, the interaction between type and image, and the flow of these elements from page to page

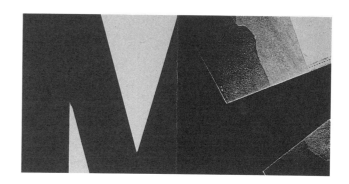

The visual flow across the pages should be strong; it should surprise and stimulate the viewer.

The students often include within their books some elements from previous letterform studies, such as the K used above.

The book begins gently and builds in intensity from page to page. After the buildup, we have to come down; we must design a conclusion that does not leave the viewer stranded.

It is like climbing a hill. After reaching the top, we can roll, fall, bounce, jump, or slide down. We can even walk down.

A set of pages showing progression of form from left to right and right to left.

The students are led to appreciate serious photographers, past and present, who are particularly interested in form: Man Ray, the Westons, Herbert Matter, Stieglitz, Steichen, Walker Evans, Cartier Bresson; they also discover Harry Callahan and Aaron Siskind. The works of photographers like Blondeau, Giacomelli, Jachna, Josephson, Larson, and Wood also nicely fit this project.

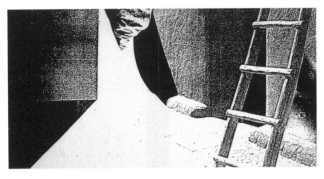

Double-page spread.

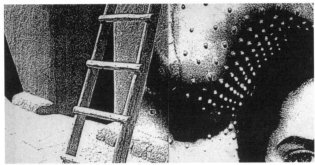

A right-hand page and the one that follows when the page is turned.

Double-page spread.

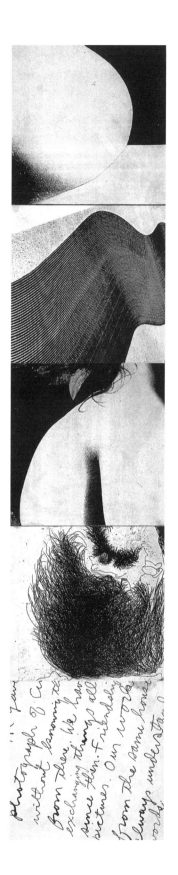

The students don't choose all of their images in the first round of research; they return to their sources several times.

The assignment leads to discussion about why most books lack the energy that these projects have and how the interior qualities of an image often require more freedom in the placement of that image than a strict grid system allows. We usually end with a lament about the common book production practice of making windows for photos before they are chosen and dropping them into place without regard for their visual connection to the type around them.

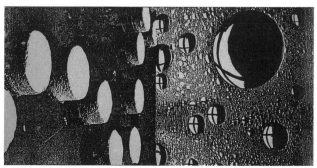

An accordion folded book.

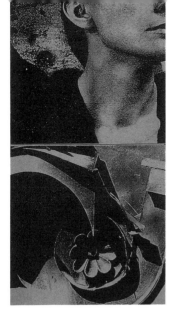

The books unfold to reveal a rich variety of forms.

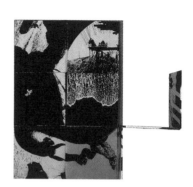

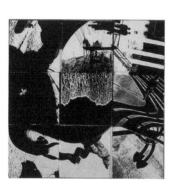
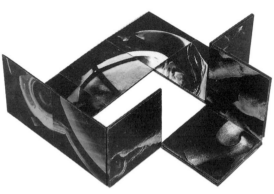

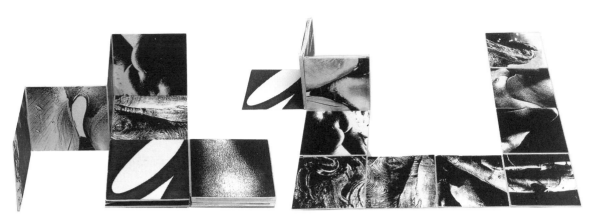

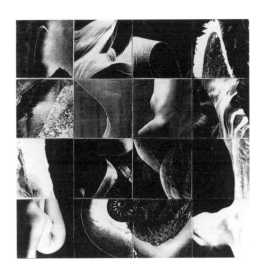

These books are composed of sixteen square panels hinged to unfold in a spiral fashion. Photographic images are placed on the front and back of each panel, making a total of thirty-two pages.

The images must progress and relate to one another in all directions, horizontal, vertical, diagonal, front to back, and when the book is opened to make a 3/D form. The overall composition should feel coherent, all of a piece. A demanding, provocative exercise, to say the least.

At the beginning of this exercise, most students doubt that they can meet the challenge. At the end, they usually feel a great sense of satisfaction.

A Structural Framework

Here we take a double-page spread from the last assignment and place upon it a grid that can establish guidelines for rearranging parts of the original composition.

As the students alter the layout, they must remain loyal to the grid although structure should not overpower the original pattern of elements.

When done successfully, the rearranged composition takes on new dimensions.

Using the grid in this way develops an awareness of the virtues of visual structure, making the composition more active and vivid.

This assignment is not as easy as it may appear. It takes sensitive control to stop rearranging before the composition becomes overworked and loses freshness. Color, form, texture, contrasts, and blending, all must be considered.

It usually takes students several attempts to reach a successful solution.

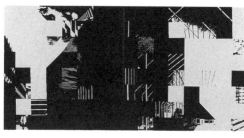

Juxtaposing Images

Simple illustrations are used to show how "reality" can be distorted by juxtaposition of images. If we look into a city and see two people in a fistfight, and if we document this from a distance with a camera, the shot shows a fight taking place in a city. If we zoom in, we can make it seem that the entire population is fighting. If we juxtapose that photograph with stacked guns, we can make it seem that something even more serious is taking place.

By juxtaposing images we can make people think that certain things are taking place when, in fact, they are not. These strategies can be used for good or bad purposes. A photographer in the sixties took photographs of university students marching about carrying placards. Six students were marching; others were having picnics, reading, throwing frisbees. This person photographed the whole scene the way he saw it but was told by his superiors, "We want it to look as though the whole campus is reacting." He refused, though he believed in the marching students' cause, and he lost his job. Another photographer was sent to take his place; the final combination of article and photographs made it appear that the whole campus had turned out in protest.

The magazine's portrayal of the student uprising exaggerated to the point of fantasy. We can rationalize that the purpose is good and the images actual. If we are disgusted with dishonesty in advertising we should be more so when journalism distorts the truth.

Visual Connections

We construct the framework for an
8″ × 8″ cube and cover one half of each
side with a rectangular panel. Looking
through the cube, the front panel is on
the left half of the front cube face; the
back one is on the right.

Photographic images similar in form
but different in content are juxtaposed,
one to each panel.

The empty spaces between the panels
become a counterform to the panels
themselves.

As you spin the cube on its diagonal
axis, the visual form and space should
pulsate without any image dominating.

The effect suggests a Möbius strip: no
beginning or end.

We discuss the importance of visual relationships among components and empty
space when constructing exhibits. We
consider how, in many ways, an exhibit
is like a book; you can go back and
forth at your own pace.

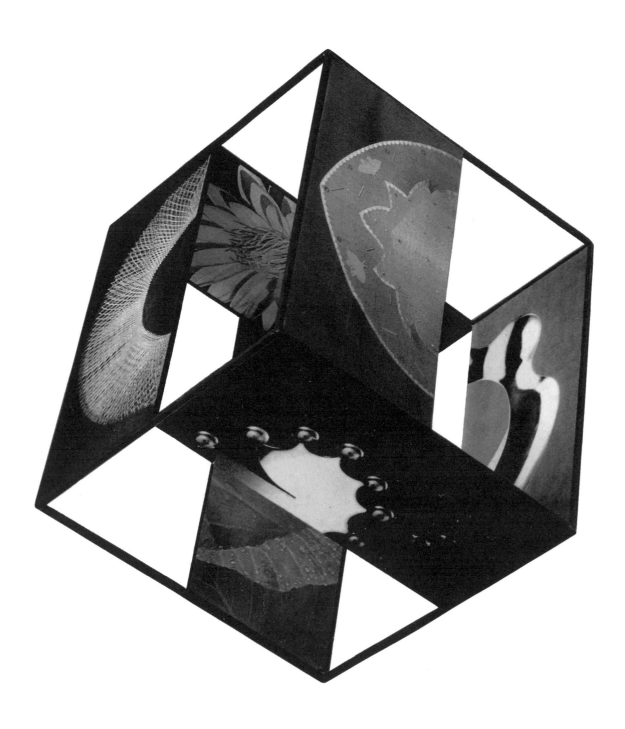

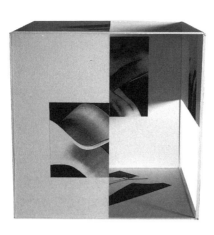

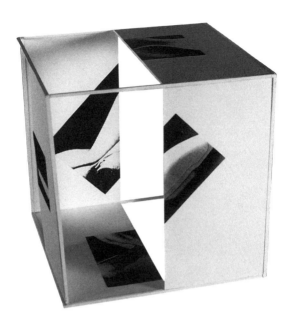

New visual relationships emerge when the
cube is rotating.

Overview

Part way through the course, I ask each student to design an overview of work done up to that point.

This exercise requires a review of assignments and helps reveal the unity within a diversity of tasks; it also prompts reflections upon the relationship between this course and the rest of their curriculum.

They can produce the overview in the form of a three-dimensional system (like the cube assignment) or a poster or a book.

Ten Steps

Since the outset of my teaching career, I have given various assignments based on ten parts or steps.

Sometimes I ask for ten stages in the evolution of a particular shape or object. Or the series can consist of ten images unrelated in content but unified by some visual attribute.

Here the students bring into play principles and processes they have studied and applied in previous assignments: such things as figure/ground, field in motion, balance, form progression, and spatial connections.

The students respond to this ten-step challenge with inventive delight. I have a large collection of such sequences, covering an astonishing range of effects, charming, troubling, funny, bizarre, startling.

I am not certain how I arrived at the magic number ten. It's not too few, not too many. It gives a starting point and structure for teacher and student, with lots of room for imaginative expression within an arbitrary scheme.

This project, from one to ten, is an exercise in flow and progression.

The students can use ten pages in book form or a series of ten separate plates. The pages or plates are numbered from one to ten.

Each time I encounter these ten-step projects I experience them in a slightly different way. This is true of much in life. It is true of certain people, rooms, a lot of art.

Students routinely approach these ten-step problems with great attention and precision. There is something in us that likes a series.

In the series on the right, each number overlaps with and becomes part of the next. Number one fuses with number two, two becomes part of three, and so on.

Hinged pages that fold out, revealing unexpected parts of the next number.

This example is designed as an accordion-fold book. The student has taken advantage of previous studies in form and counterform and in form progression.

The double-page spreads can be shifted. Even though normal books have odd numbered pages on the right, in this example, you have a choice. Also, the design wraps around the outside edges of the pages.

Next is a series emphasizing dimension, color,
reflection, and movement.

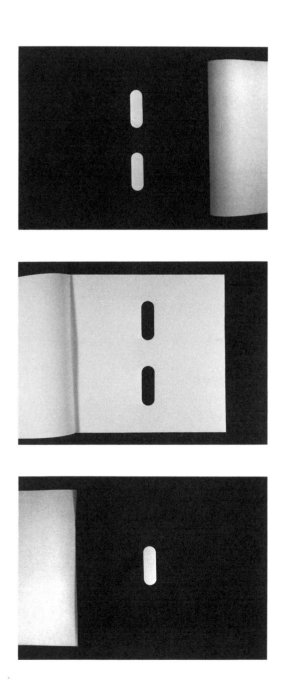

The number of bicyclists forms this series. The
number of riders increases page by page.
Their placement expresses movement. Riders
race across each page.

 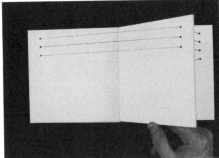 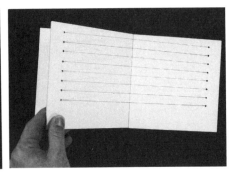

This is a continuous string that makes a soft, engaging sound as you open the pages. The string laces through the pages, representing each number in turn. As the lighting varies so do the shadows cast by the strings.

In this book the shapes rise to present constantly changing colors reflecting on other colors as the shapes move to full extension.

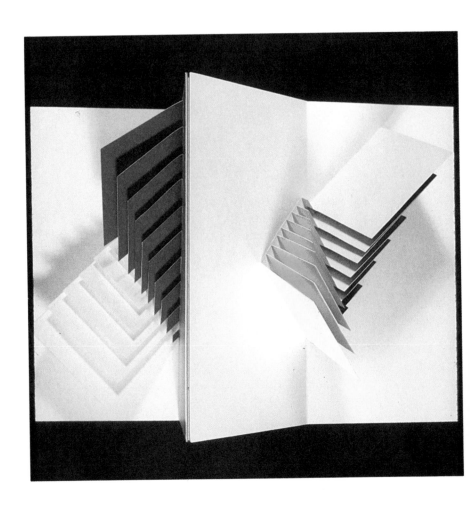

The book's pages are mirrored surfaces that vary reflections as the angle of viewing varies. The angle is controlled by a string at the top corners.

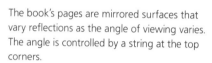

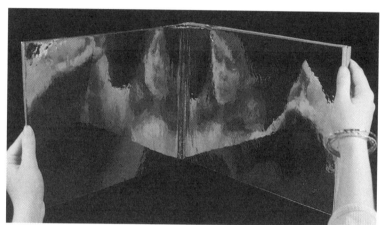

A series of ten folded covers containing pockets holding from one to ten loosely folded units that do not come out unless removed with the pages closed. Gravity pulls the loose pieces to the side that is down, showing variable color from side to side. The mixtures of color are always changing, glowing.

Function of a Handtool

Demonstrate the function of a handtool, using an assigned number of steps and photograms. If a pencil is the chosen theme, then imagine that your audience has never seen a pencil and has no concept of its use. Employ no unnecessary steps, only those important to the message. Repetition may sometimes be necessary. The main task is to avoid inessentials; develop a story line and stick to it.

The compass demonstrates and explains itself by performing a little dance.

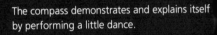

In this example, pattern suggests the tension and movement of a magnetic field. The nails and magnet are dynamically interacting components.

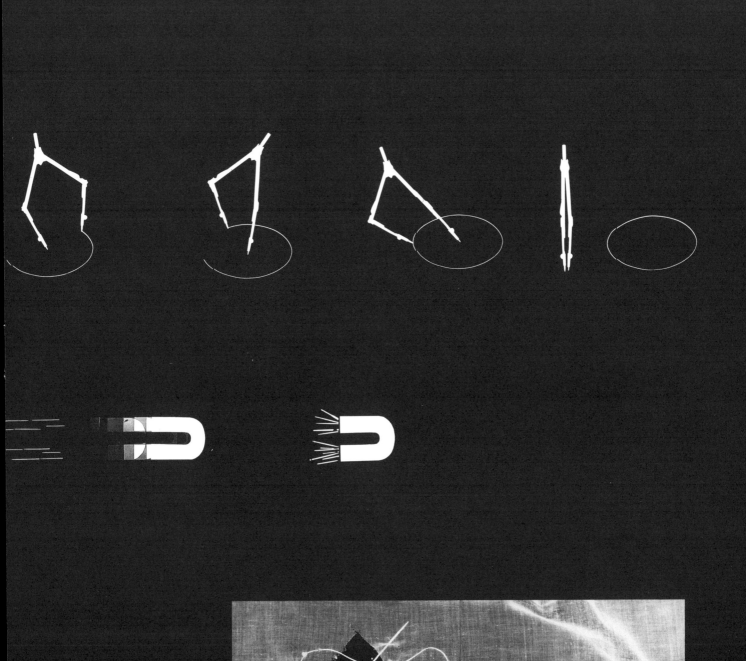

In these examples, the strongest statements are the simplest.

A poetic relationship between a handtool and other objects.

The pruning sheers proudly say, "Here I am." It moves forward, gets the first flower, moves back, then forward again to get the second flower.

You realize that the bastard is going to get the last one. It does; then says "Look what I did!"

If the pruning sheers were shown in proper perspective relative to the flowers, you would be viewing it from the top. The configuration would be realistic but boring.

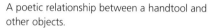

The zipper takes advantage of the book as it zips up the pages.

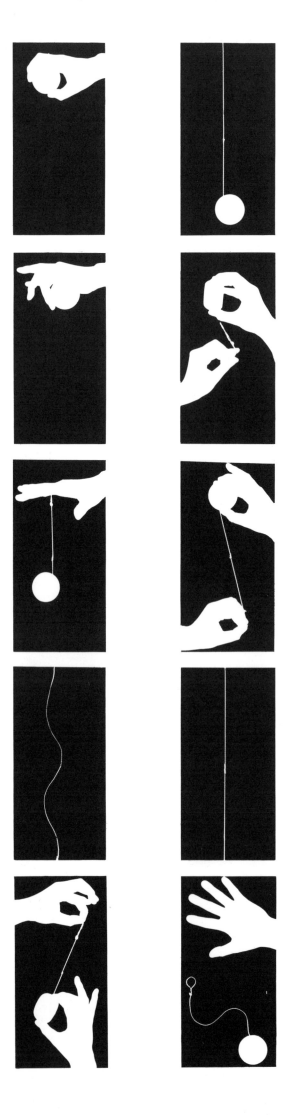

It is difficult to make a photogram of an active hand. Its gestures must be exaggerated to be convincing. (A photogram is formed by placing an object on photosensitive paper and exposing it to light. When the paper is "developed," an image of the object appears in negative form.)

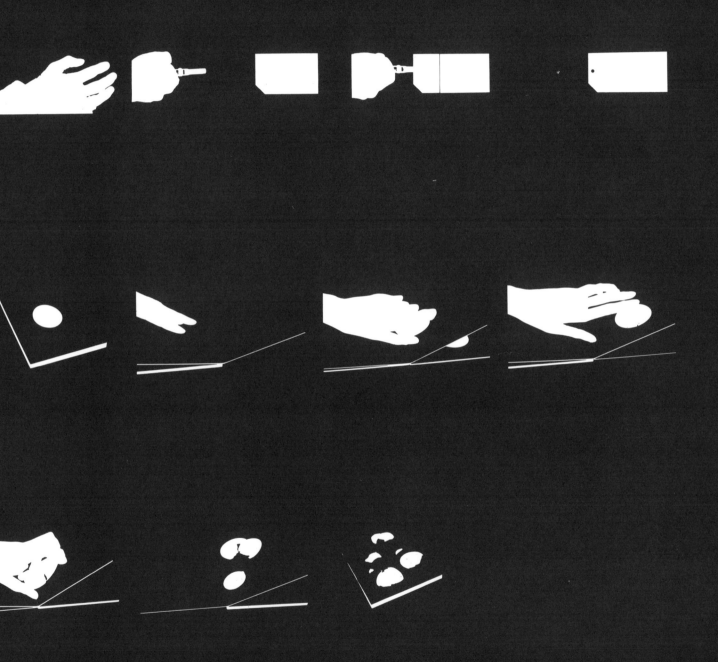

Once the plane has established itself and its action, it leaves the scene and the shavings take over.

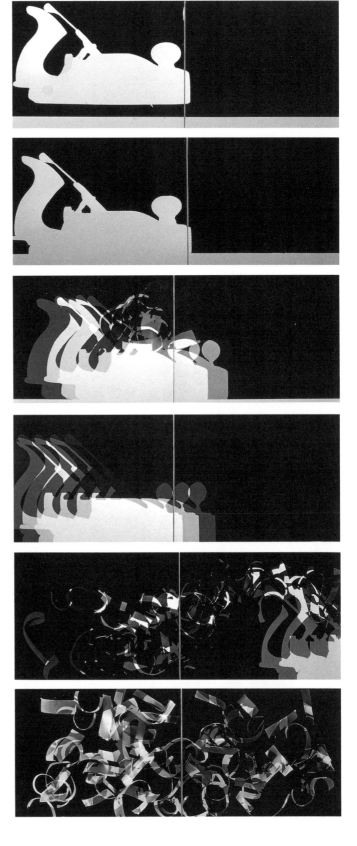

Extensions of the assignment.

In this example, we see a still life that won't stay still. The problem: To focus attention on a pencil that is drawing and erasing itself.

This project combines photograms and photographs, an intriguing relationship between the handtool and human action.

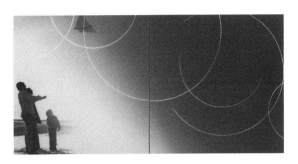

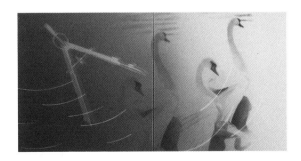

Combining Visual Stories

Another level of information is added to the handtool assignment; a second story, documented by photographs, is included.

The messages work independently, do not duplicate each other; but together they are convincing.

The second story adds to the book, makes it more interesting.

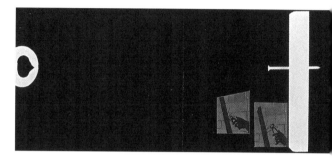

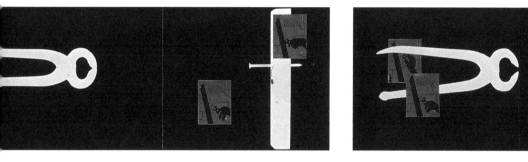

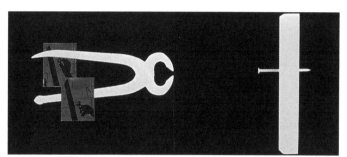

This is another exercise in ten steps, a progression that transmutes a letterform into an entirely new thing. Step one is assigned; step ten could be anything. The steps must be even. You may get to step six and realize that you have to start over to avoid unevenness or tedium.

When you open a book, you see two pages side by side. A book forms a rhythm of twos. Each step must cover a double-page spread. When you look at the very beginning of a book, your eye probably settles on the right hand page.

It then moves back and forth across the spread. This dynamic must be kept in mind as the student invents the ten-step transformation.

As the letter undergoes its metamorphosis, it can twist, stretch, change scale, shape, and position from spread to spread. The images appear to move as pages are turned.

These exercises bring vitality and humor to my classroom. Not because of me, but because of the students' vigor and their joy in the act of creation.

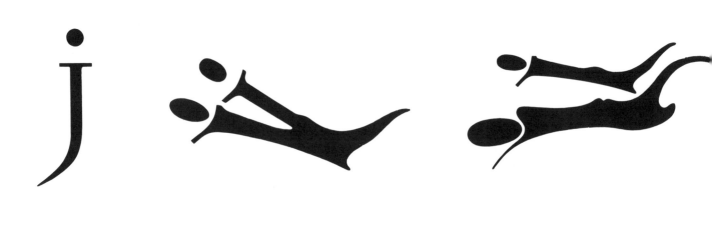

A Word's Meaning Visualized

In advancing steps, the word explains itself.

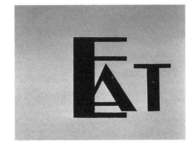

"Eat," after eating, passes some of what it ate.

Letters are drawn and combined with organic forms.

Visual Comparisons

The following four assignments relate organic and man-made forms.

The letter and its companion each assert the qualities of the other.

Placement of the letter on the double-page spread should reveal its inner form, which might otherwise be overlooked.

These assignments are arranged in book form in a sequence of double-page spreads. The photographs, which may be cropped, are presented in a straightforward manner. The letters should be placed to draw the viewer's attention to the area in the photograph that the designer wants to emphasize. The book should have a consistent mood throughout, its sequence moving smoothly from page to page.

These exercises illustrate how design can establish mood and direct attention.

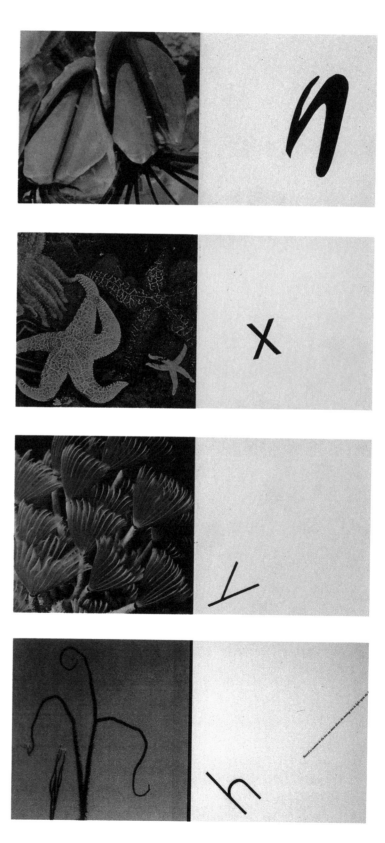

Select or take a photograph showing an
architectural form that resonates with a
particular letter.

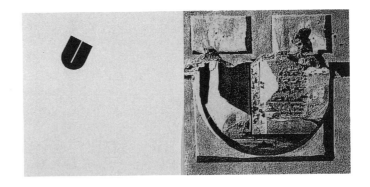

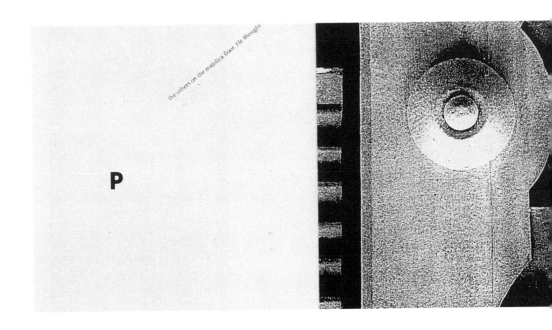

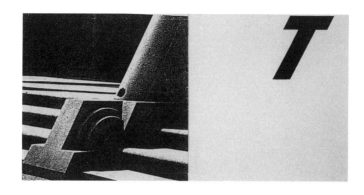

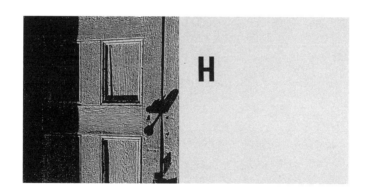

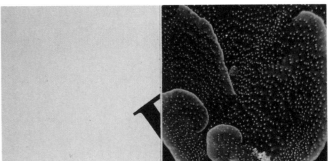

The student draws an addition to the photograph, thereby generating a letterform,
adding another layer of information, making
the double-page spreads more active.

 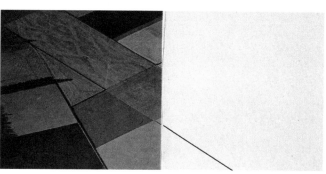

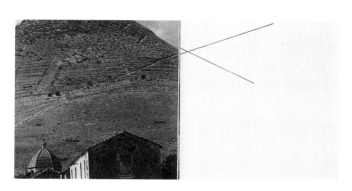 

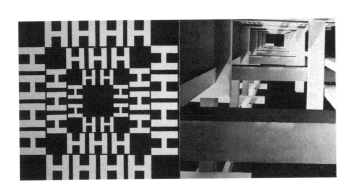

Relating patterns of letterforms and other man-made forms.

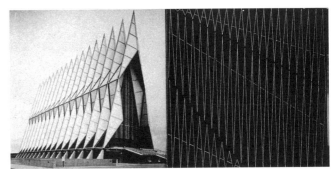

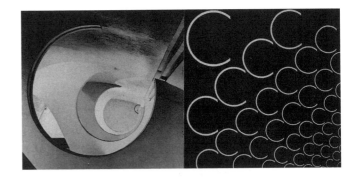

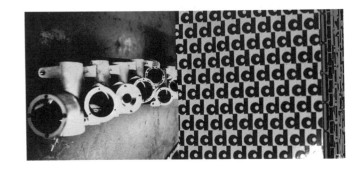

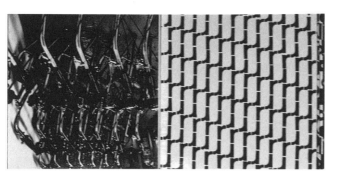

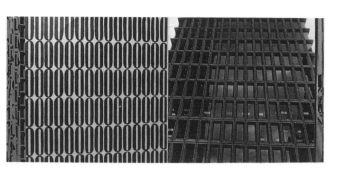

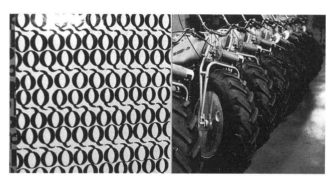

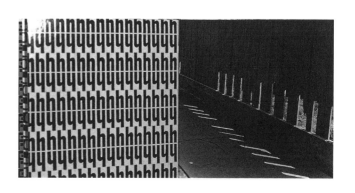

The same photograph is used in each case but
the letterforms differ; size and placement of
the drawn letter help reveal the complimen-
tary form within the photograph.

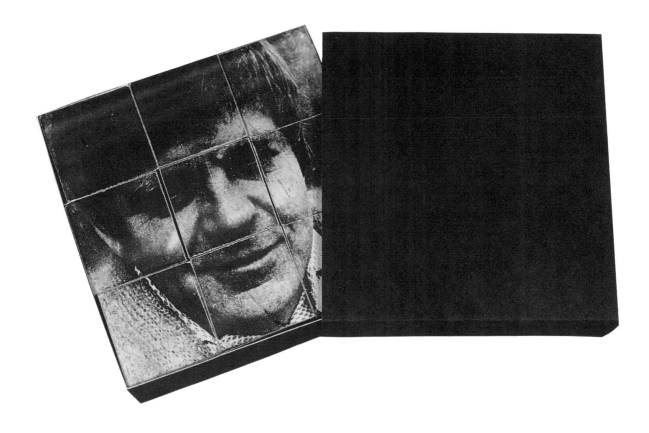

This example, using moveable noses, is a play
on similarities and differences.

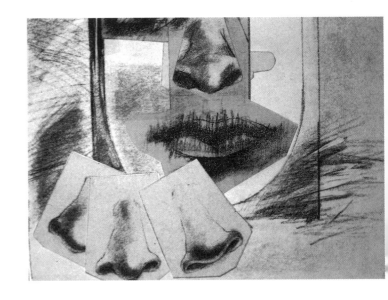

Variations on a Theme

As with the previous assignment, these three-dimensional projects, consisting of moveable parts, are studies in the formation of relationships among components.

In this case, human features are the theme.

This project, a study in genealogy, is based on ten related parts. Nine cubes form a rectangle representing the tenth part. The front and back surfaces of the form contain photographic images of the students' parents. Thirty-six other surfaces are covered with facial features of the rest of the family. By changing the cubes, you are able to see relationships among genetically determined traits: shapes of noses, cleft chins, dimples, and other facial structures.

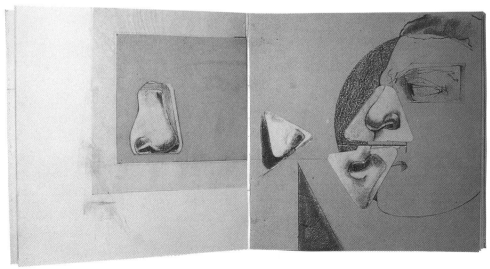

Analyzing Form

Take a simple, small object, one we usually accept without much thought, and study its form.

Study its structure, texture, and color.

In this example, we can think of the thumbtack as point (the sharp end), line (the shaft), and circle (the head). One also sees an ellipse, various curves, shadows, reflections, many colors, and many motions in response to forces, whether physical—magnetic or gravitational or whatever—or perceptual.

Document these investigations with drawing and photography. The variations should fit into thematic groups.

This kind of study leads students to examine the intricate world around us. We can't sustain this degree of sensitivity indefinitely without exhausting our senses. But now and then a close look brings pleasures and insight. Designers need the exercise.

In the very early stages of this assignment, students realize that alternative "solutions" to the design problem are endless in number. There really is a universe in a grain of sand.

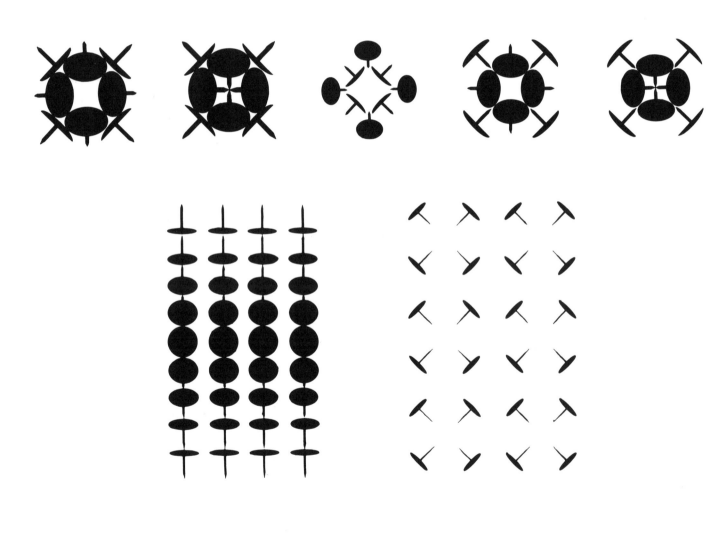

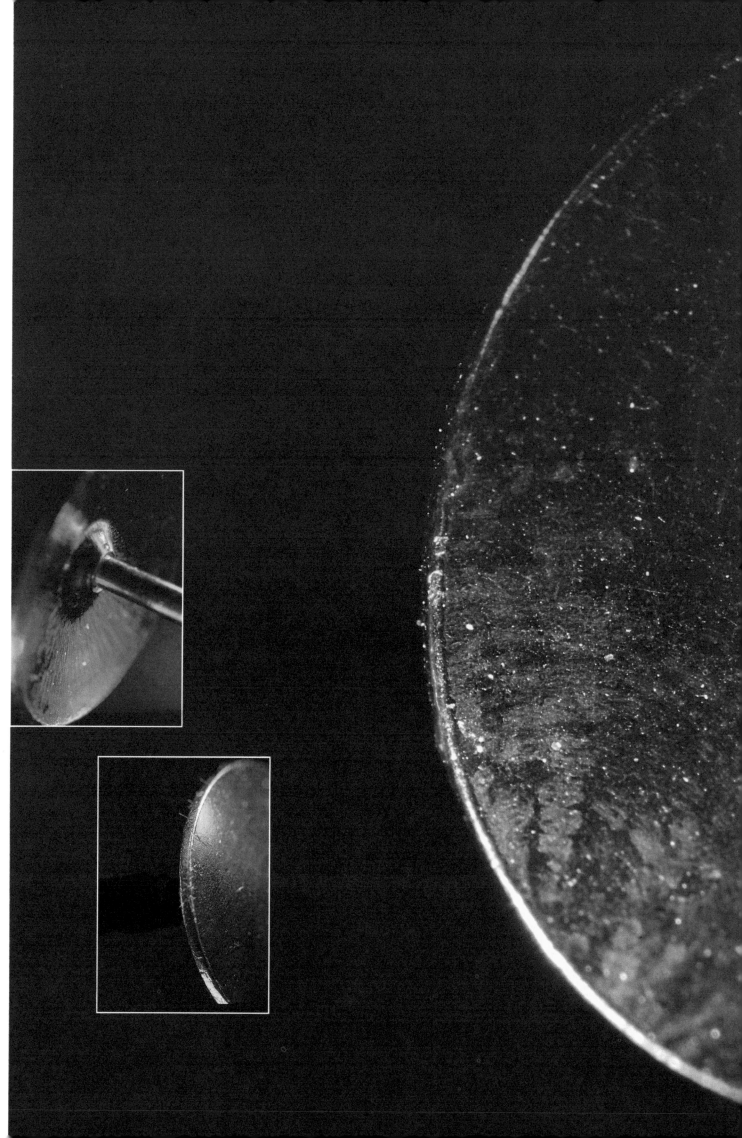

Nesting boxes. This structure changes in form and mood as the angle from which it is viewed is changed.

One to Ten

Design and build a three-dimensional form with ten expandable and retractable parts. These constructions are used to change the appearance of an architectural space.

Placement in an environment should be such that the formal qualities of the construction are enhanced.

Once the construction is in place, the next step is to document, through photography, any changes that occur in the appearance of the environment owing to placement of the construction.

Viewpoint, light, and shadow strongly influence the viewer's experience.

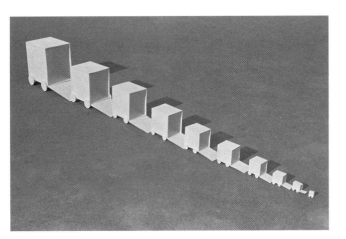

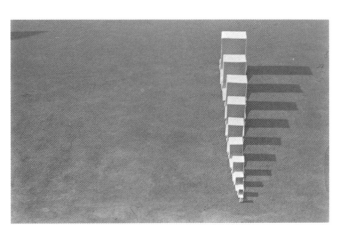

Essence of an Object

For this assignment, we again choose commonplace objects.

A single item is given to each student. They are encouraged to allow the object to act on them freely, to take the leading role.

The students begin to express themselves verbally and visually. I try to move them beyond their initial point of view; they end up moving well beyond my own. Eventually they are all involved in each others' work.

This kind of assignment is challenging for teacher and students, since its success depends largely on spontaneous enthusiasm and imagination. There are no design manuals from which to draw guidance. The process evolves unpredictably.

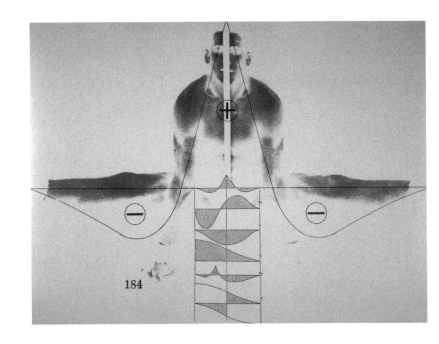

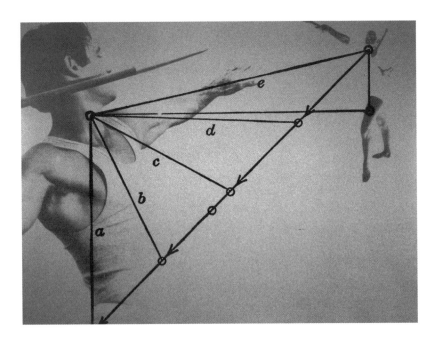

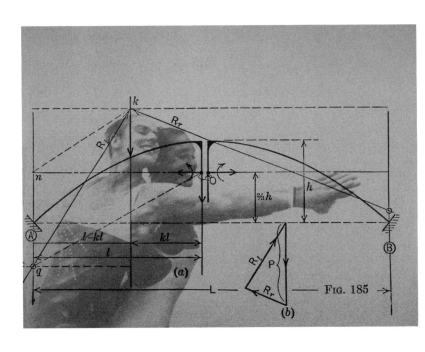

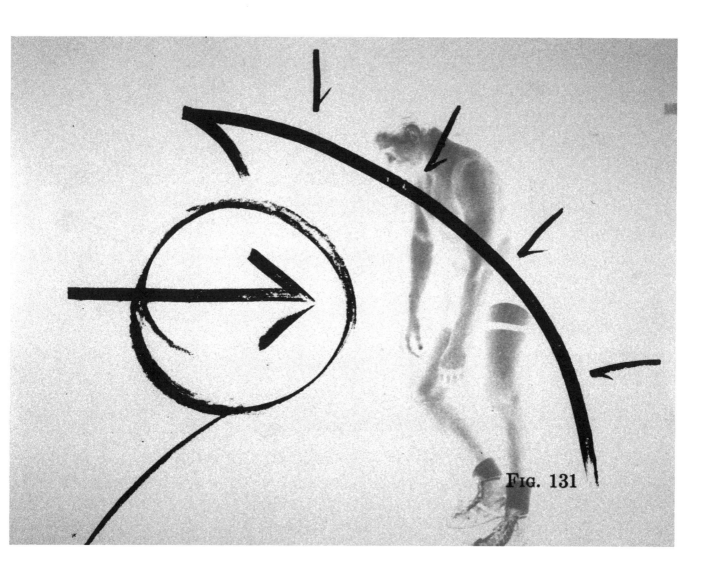

FIG. 131

The student is handed a rubber band and decides to explore its energy, its elasticity, instead of its utilitarian purpose.

The beginning sketches stretch across a large piece of paper. Taut pencil lines move from light to dark; an even wave suggests limpness.

I smile as I write this, remembering the student's gestures, actions like a dancer's, in the enthusiasms of alternate stretching and collapsing.

The student juxtaposed the "soft" images of dance, which had been photographed, with the hard-line graphs. The work gains strength from this juxtaposition.

This example began with a small piece of
rope; it became a hangman's knot—images
of hangings, Sing-Sing prison, sing-song.
"Do your ears hang low, can you tie them in
a knot, can you tie them in a bow?"

The book took on the rhythm of the song.
Turning the pages is part of that rhythm.
The song and images die out when the book
comes to a close.

A spiral-shaped spring evolves into curls and
rams' horns.

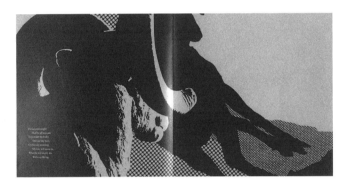

A student used romantic sweet dreams, poems, and lines from songs, such as "ladybug fly away home" and "somewhere over the rainbow, blue birds fly," in contrast to photographs of poverty in the United States.

He used xeroxed images, layers of varying contrast and density, combined and re-copied onto one surface.

I found out later that he had entered this piece in a national competition and received an award.

A stack of ten frames, each with its own mechanics, allowing portions of an image to be moved relative to one another. The whole stack fits neatly into a box. The theme is a commercial Christmas. The candy cane symbolizes that theme, but each frame, which can separately be removed from the box, shows some product that conveys the idea of a Christmas gift.

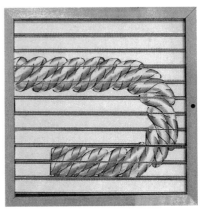

The front and back of one frame.

This frame allows fragments of a "product" to
be shifted, producing a diversity of compositions.

Shapes were cut into cardboard the size of a slide mount.

When light is projected through these cutouts into smoke, you get something of the feeling of a space container. Faulty physics but interesting design.

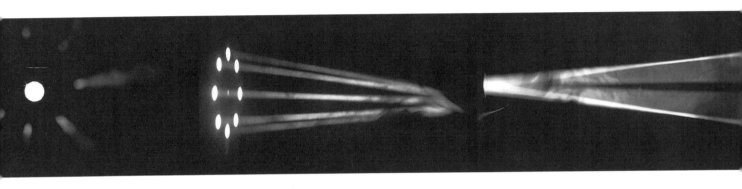

 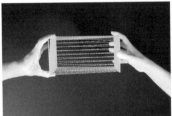 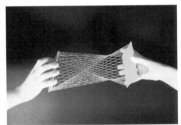

As you turn this flat square, it springs into a container-like form.

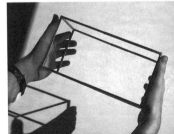  

Highly polished brass tubes that fit neatly into each other are filled with hydraulic fluid. Gaskets keep the fluid from escaping. As you press against the cube-like form, it pushes back, giving a *feeling* that space is being contained.

Containers/Contents

Design three containers, each suggesting its contents: sand, Ping-Pong balls, and space.

The container becomes an extension of the thing it contains. Consider weight, texture, form, and color.

Consider, also, the unique characteristics of the thing each container will hold. When you pour sand from one point, as the pile gets higher the angle of the sides remains the same. The sound of Ping-Pong balls rattling together has a quality all its own.

Burlap or sandpaper could contain the sand. A material that suggests lightness may be used for the Ping-Pong balls. A transparent substance could contain the space. Pressure usually becomes a factor as students invent the space container. Absolutely empty space is hard to come by here on earth. So try to design a container that gives a *sense* of containing space—and nothing else.

None of this is meant to be science. We are seeking perceptual, impressionistic effects.

A goose egg shell contains a Ping-Pong ball, which makes a distinctive rattle within.

A form made of burlap and filled with sand.

I assign a small amount of text that conveys at least two layers of meaning and encourage the students to read and re-read the words.

We discuss their interpretations at length.

A favorite passage for this assignment is a speech made in 1854 by Chief Seattle to Isaac Stevens, Governor of Washington Territory. I like its rhythm and the images it brings to mind. I like the way it switches back and forth from *we* to *you*. *We* represents the Indians; *you*, the white man. Students can consider Chief Seattle's message from a personal perspective or see it in terms of history, sociology, anthropology, ecology, or whatever. Either way, it lends itself to evocative design.

Design a visual expression of the text.

Design the typography.

Design a piece that combines type and image.

  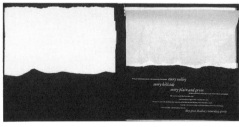

Sixteen chairs are arranged in sequence, with emphasis on the numbers one through sixteen. Explore typographic possibilities within a grid.

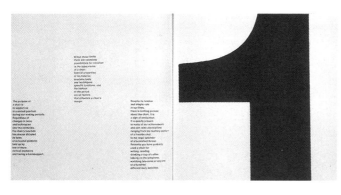

The purpose of
a chair is
to support us
in a seated posture
during our waking periods.

Dining Chair 1946
Molded plywood with Walnut Veneer and
impregnated masonite finish, rubber, steel mounts.
Designed by Charles Eames. Amer. b. 1907

American Side Chair
19th century
mahogany horsehair seat
from the Stewart Family Homestead,
Coxsackie, New York,
lent by Mrs. Julian Clark

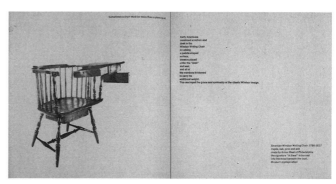

Sometimes a chair must be more than a place to sit.

American Windsor Writing Chair 1790-1817
maple, oak, pine and ash
made by Arthur Shaw of Philadelphia
the signature "A.Shaw" is burned
into the wood beneath the seat.
Museum appropriation

Although no original
examples survive,
the klismos
in its perfected
form appears
in Greek vase painting,
most often
in domestic scenes.

A a *a* a **B** *b* b b C
c c **c** D *d* **d** **d** **E** e
e e F *f* **f** f **G** g g
g H **h** h *h* **I** i **i** **i**
J **j** **j** *j* **K** k *k* *k* L
l *1* 1 **M** *m* m **m** **N** n
n n O o *0* *o* P **p** *p*
p Q *q* *q* **q** **R** **r** *r* r
S s s *s* T *t* t t U
u *u* **u** V **v** **v** *v* W **w**
w *w* X **x** *x* **x** **Y** y *y*
y Z **z** z **z** **z** z *z* **z**

Letterforms and Typography

Every letter is not necessarily beautiful when judged as a single unit. Each letter is companion to twenty-five others; some are symmetrical, others asymmetrical. The beauty of a letter is revealed by how it meshes with companion parts of a total typographic system, how it works in combination with its fellows.

Single letterforms combine to form words, which form sentences, which form paragraphs, and so on up to books and beyond. Each typeface has its own texture and tone. Students of typography begin their studio course by studying the makeup of single letterforms, examining their inner parts.

There are no hard and fast rules for typography any more than there are such rules for painting pictures. Sensible students will learn about the typography of the past as well as the present, even though they can enjoy the privilege of ignoring either in their future work.

An understanding of traditional faces seems particularly urgent since technology continues to exert strong influence on typography. Not all of these influences are good. Many typefaces available today have been designed by technologists who have only slight background in the arts or typography. It is easy, maybe too easy, to design a typeface on the computer screen.

Several hundred typefaces have been designed; only a few measure up to classic standards of readability, balance, harmony—timeless qualities, not just vogue.

I favor no particular process or style—hot or cold type, hand or machine set, formal or informal, classic or modern. I propose for students a developing study of letterforms and typestyles; families of typefaces; thick, thin, bold and light; serifs and san serifs.

For the graphic designer typography involves technology and craft, expressing action and a state of being.

Sometimes I spend hours choosing a typeface to suit a particular situation.

I have to use a typeface several times before I learn to use it effectively, according, of course, to my aesthetics.

A beautiful typeface is not always the "right" one. Subtleties count. I may feel the ascenders or descenders are wrong for the job at hand; density may accumulate in the wrong place; a crossed "w" may give too much weight in a particular location. These nuances are matters of taste; but so are notes in music and colors in painting. A trained eye will discern more than the naive eye. So I bring students into the details, where the devils and angels dwell.

Choosing a typeface is not entirely arbitrary. Each typeface is suited to only certain kinds of information and purpose. If we are designing typographic layouts for a novel or textbook, they are likely to differ from typography that works for a single-page announcement.

There are some typefaces that I dislike. It would be foolish to say that I would never use them. I may end up using one tomorrow. In design, all rules are springboards into realms beyond the rules.

To my mind, beautiful typography is based on selection of a typeface in resonance with the text, the sensitive use of space between letters and words, the length of lines and their alignments, the space between lines and between paragraphs, and the placement of type on the page. The overall effect further depends on clear typographic delineation of the different levels of information, the color, light, and texture of the type as it sits on the page, the paper on which it is printed, and the quality of the printing.

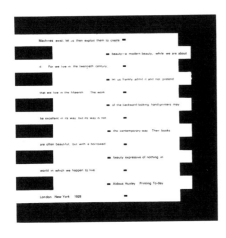

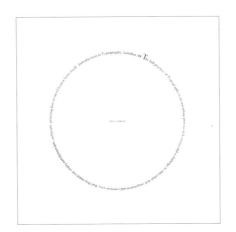

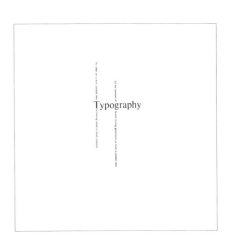

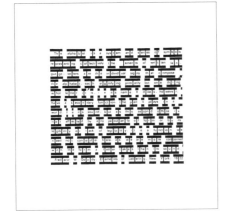

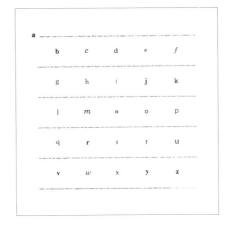

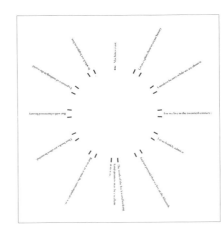

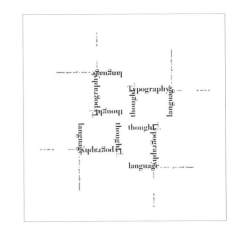

Typographic Form

At the beginning of this class, I assign a warm-up exercise based solely on typography; no pictures.

As an example, I pass out several philosophical statements written by outstanding typographers.

Each student must choose a certain number of these, let's say eight, design a series of plates, and present them in a folio. I normally assign a square format, larger than usual, usually sixteen by sixteen inches.

Through their design, the students can demonstrate support for the statements or react against them.

Their first step is to sketch ideas using a chosen typeface; the second is to refine the initial concept into a typographic layout; the third is to write specifications for typesetting; the fourth is typesetting itself. Most students use the computer for this setting, although in each class there is usually at least one student who loves the texture of type on paper and will hand-set the type in metal. That student probably learns more about the subtleties of typography than can be learned by using a computer. These sharpened sensitivities can later be applied to electronic composition.

Most students enter the school knowing how to use a computer; very few will have the typographic knowledge to apply this tool effectively.

The last step is to print a number of copies of this folio.

Various assignments can serve as warm-up exercises: for example, a weather report or pages of a calendar.

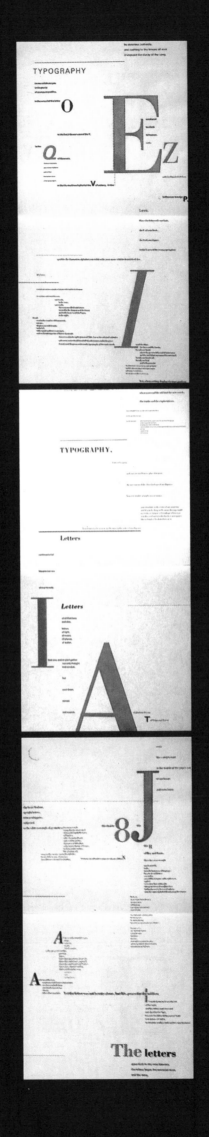

characters of Aldus firm as the
marine stature of Venice,
in whose mother waters,
like a leaning sail,
navigates the
cursive curving the alphabet:
the air of the oceanic discovers
slanted forever
the profile of writing.
From medieval hands to your eye
advanced this
N
this double
8
this
J
this
R   of rey and ricio.
There they were wrought much as
teeth, nails, metallic hammers of language:
they beat each letter,
erected it,
a small **black** statue
on the whiteness.

A LOVE OF LETTERS

is the beginning of typographical wisdom.
That is, the love of letters as literature
and the love of letters as physical entities,
having abstract beauty of their own,
apart from the ideas they may express or
the emotion they may evoke.

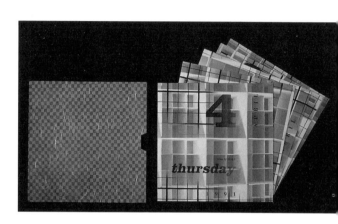

3 0th 303 1990

oCtOBer (uesday)

1

2

3

MARCH
FRIDAY
16TH
DAY OF
YEAR
1990

8

5

A selection of 6″ × 9″ pages designed by students, based on the poem *Fireworks* by Elizabeth Jennings.

The purpose of this exercise is to devise a typographic form responsive to the message in the text.

Every student leaves class with a bound book containing a page from each classmate.

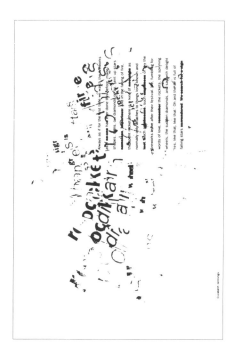

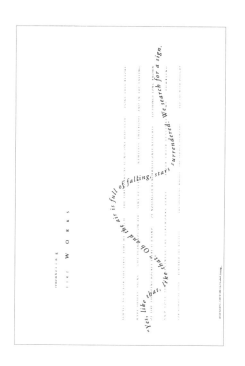

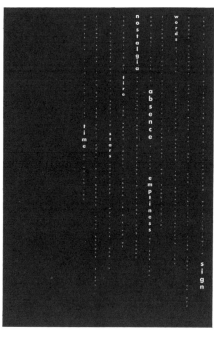

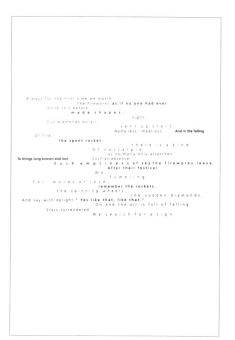

A typographic exercise displaying greetings, from over fifty countries, that were sent into outer space in hopes that they will be received by intelligent life elsewhere in our galaxy or beyond.

Be healthy—I greet you.
Russian Best wishes to you all. Wu We **in**
this world send you our good will. Thai Greetings from t**he**
inhabitants of this world. Hindi To all those who exist in the universe, greeting**s.**
Armenian Greetings. On behalf of Kannada-speaking people, "good wishes". Kannada **Hi.**
How are you? Wish you peace, health and happiness. Cantonese Peace to y**0**u. We the inhabitants o**f**
this earth send our greetings to you. Urdu How are you? Korean Greetings to the inhabitants of the univer**se**
from the third planet Earth of the star the Sun. Orlya Wishing you a peaceful future from the earthlings**!**
Have you eaten yet? Come visit us if you have time. Nepali May all be well. Sumerian Peace and **happiness**
to all. Portuguese Greeting from a human being of the earth. Please contact Gujarati May all be very well. Akkadi**an**
Greetings to everybody. Romanian Good day to the entire world. French Peace Hebrew Hello and greetings to all. Spani**sh**
Hope everyone's well. We are thinking about you all. Please come here to visit us when you have time. Mandar**in**
Chinese Hello! Let there be peace everywhere. Bengali Greetings to you, whoever you are. We come in friendshi**p to**
those who are friends. Greek We wish you everything good from our planet. serbian Good night **l**adies an**d**
gentlemen. Goodbye and see you next time. Indonesian Hello to everybody from this Earth. in Kechua langua**ge.**Kechua
Hail. Hittite Hello to everyone. We are happy here and you be happy there. Rajasthani We are sending greetings **from**
our world, wishing you happiness, good health and many years. Ukranian Greetings to you, whoever you are: **we**
have good will towards you and bring peace across space. Latin Peace Aramaic Greetings. The people of t**he**
Earth send their good wishes. Marathi Heartfelt greetings to everyone. Dutch Hello to the residents of fa**r**
skies. Persian Heartfelt greetings to all. German Hello. How are you? Japanese Sincerely send yo**u**
our friendly greetings.Vietnamese Dear Turkish-speaking friends, may the honors of th**e**
morningbe upon your heads. Turkish Good health to you now and forever.
Welsh Many greetings snd wishes. Italian We greet you, **O**
great ones. Sotho Welcome, creature**s**
from beyond

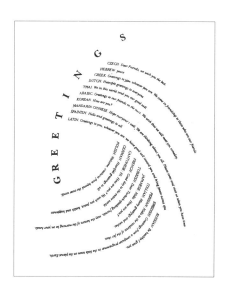

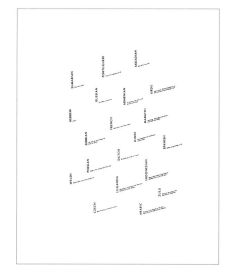

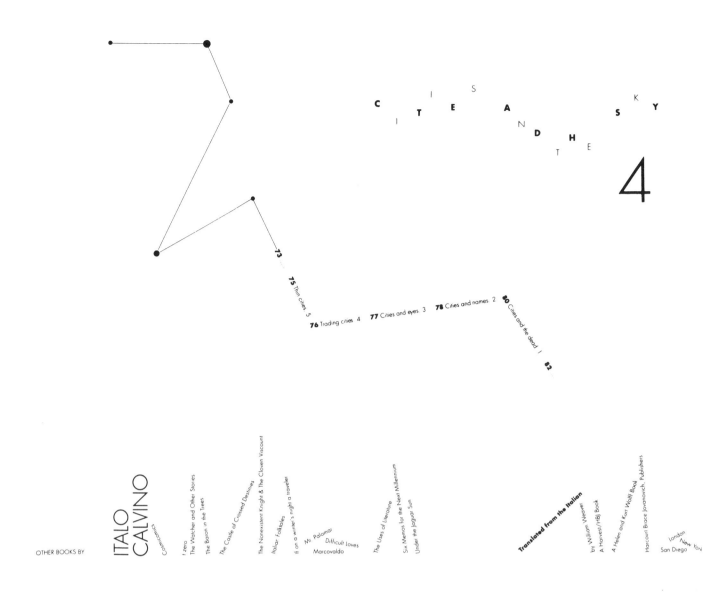

CITIES AND THE SKY

4

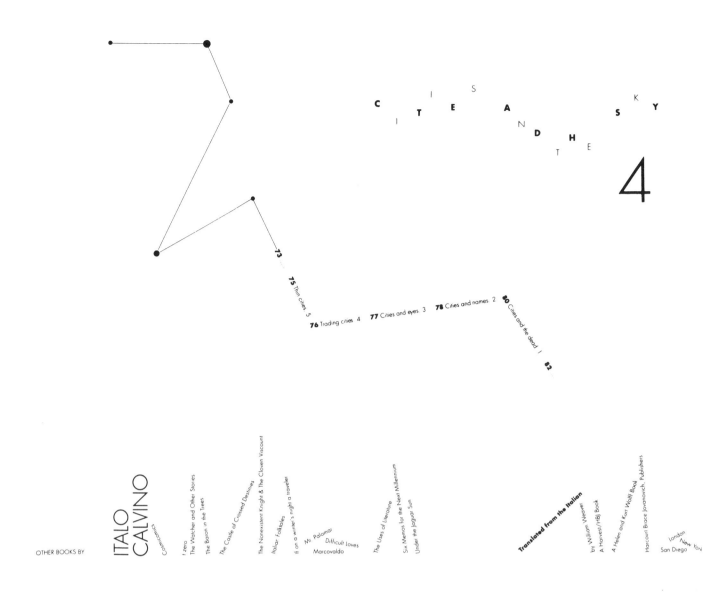

73

75 Thin Cities 5

76 Trading cities 4   **77** Cities and eyes 3   **78** Cities and names 2   **80** Cities and the dead 1

82

OTHER BOOKS BY ITALO CALVINO

Cosmicomics
t zero
The Watcher and Other Stories
The Baron in the Trees
The Castle of Crossed Destinies
The Nonexistent Knight & The Cloven Viscount
Italian Folktales
If on a winter's night a traveler
Mr. Palomar
Difficult Loves
Marcovaldo
The Uses of Literature
Six Memos for the Next Millennium
Under the Jaguar Sun

Translated from the Italian
by William Weaver
A Harvest/HBJ Book
A Helen and Kurt Wolff Book
Harcourt Brace Jovanovich, Publishers
London
New York
San Diego

Finally he comes to
ISIDORA
A city where
the buildings have
spiral
staircases
encrusted
with
spiral
seashells
where perfect
telescopes
and violins
are made
where the
foreigner
hesitating
between two
women always
encounters
a third

In the square there
is the wall where
the old men sit and
watch the young
go by, he is seated
in a row with them

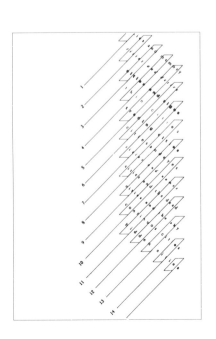

In this example we use *Invisible Cities* by Italo Calvino because of its intriguing imagery.

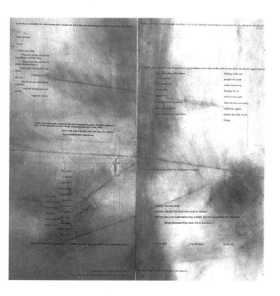

A typographic assignment showing a hierarchy of information.

Art catalogues containing such things as a half-title page, title page, copyright information, lenders list, preface, a poem, introduction, text, captions, checklist, biography, and bibliography.

I supply the students with a computer disk containing a complete manuscript.

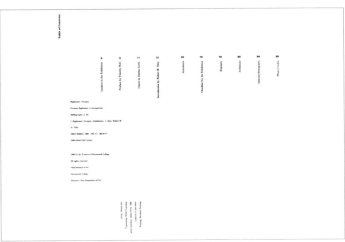

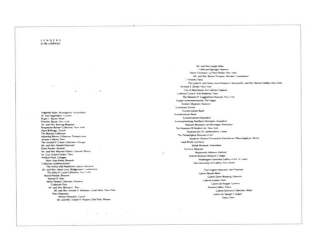

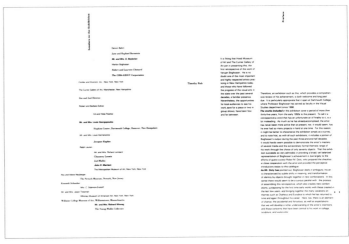

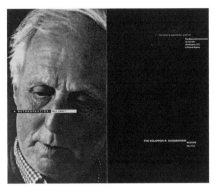

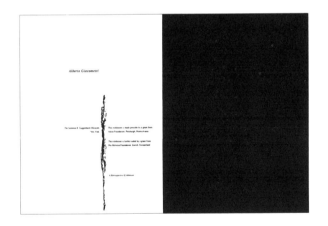

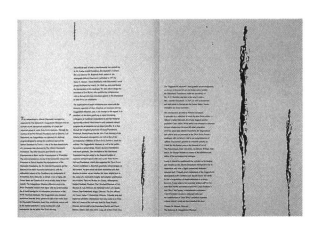

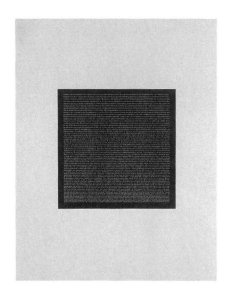

A typographic exercise using the text, not the pictures, from Aaron Siskind's *Harlem Document*. (Aaron did the photographs in the 1930s; the text was written by various people under the Federal Writers Project.)

The students choose two short stories from *Harlem Document*, each very different from the other but related by social implications.

The students design a plate for each of the two stories.

They then combine the two plates into a single, unified piece.

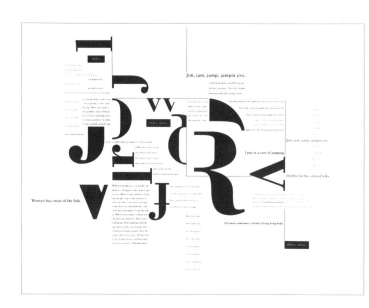

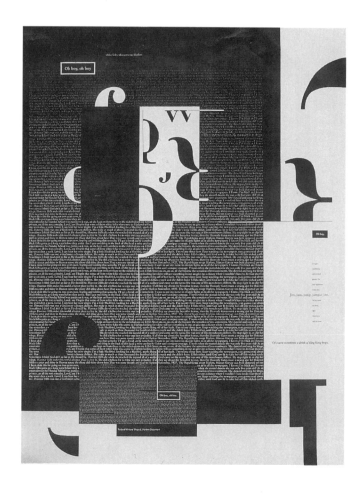

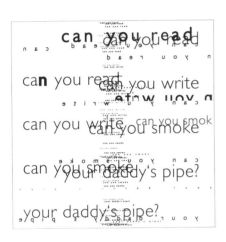

The challenge here is to construct two compositions, each conveying a particular kind of information, and then to combine these compositions into a unified version that allows the essence of each to remain clear while showing a congenial interaction between the two.

The students succeed in this effort only if they understand the content and mood of each text that serves as source and inspiration for their compositions. So they really get into this material, reading it over and over again, discussing the meanings among themselves. Their typography, of course, grows out of their understanding. The understanding comes first.

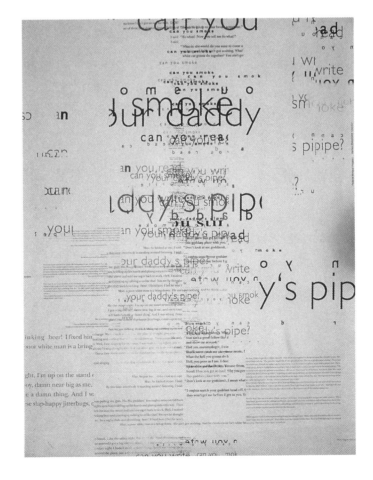

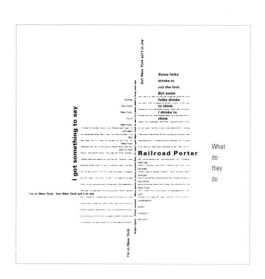

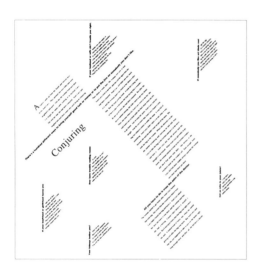

If all or most results from a particular class end up looking similar, the teacher is probably placing too much emphasis on a particular typographic style instead of encouraging the students to loosen up and invent.

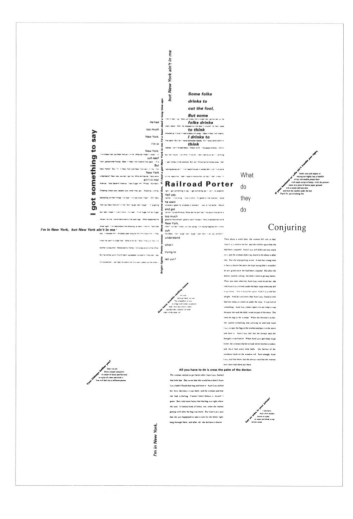

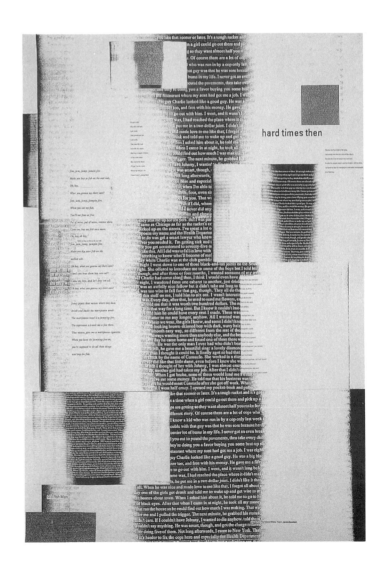

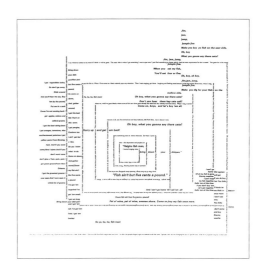

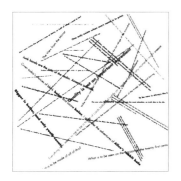

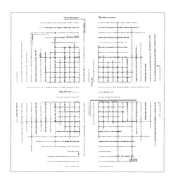

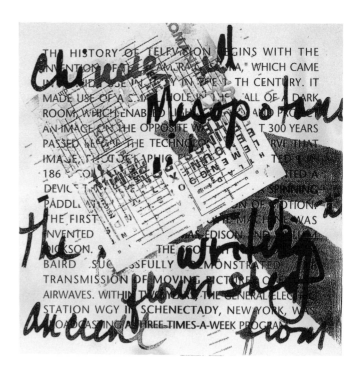

The students had to choose three separate, unrelated texts and present them in apt typographic form. The first text, on pages 150 and 151, is a set of greetings sent into outer space. The second text is an essay written by Duane Michals expressing the author's fears of the approaching twenty-first century. The third text is a collection of short, historical pieces depicting technological changes throughout history. These three texts form the base for development of this assignment.

The assignment consists of four, 16" by 16" plates, using selections from each of the three texts. The fourth plate combines the first three plates, presenting the essence of the message from each individual plate.

Audubon Society of Rhode Island

A nonprofit organization working for protection and management of the natural environment and wise use of resources.

assimilation
arch
active=independent
arrow
active
america
american
bridge
accommodation
boats
across
bell
black
bird
building
clasped
hands
bind/entwining
circles
bridge
diverse
cross   international
body
countries
between   change
chain   horizon
cooperation
crossing
paths
communication   connection/connecting
eagle   heart
cultural/cultures
flags
confused
globe
community
home
care
hands

Symbols/Signs

The assignment is to design a sign that suggests a quality or fact, an image symbolizing the activity that it represents. This sign should be independent of time, not based on fashion. It should be memorable and simple and so coherent in composition that no part can be removed without diluting the whole message. No frills.

This is not a corporate identity project, although it requires a similar process. The main purpose is to design a strong, concise visual statement.

When students are asked to find an existing symbol that meets these criteria, they find it astonishing that so few exist. Later they see why. It is difficult to design a good one—it takes concentrated effort, imagination, talent.

This assignment is more demanding than designing a poster or book; you are not likely to have a preconceived notion of what the end result will be.

The students begin by doing research on the organization for which the symbol is being constructed. Members of the organization are asked to express their vision of the organization as it is now and what it can become if all goes well. The students must try to give these perceptions, dreams, and intentions symbolic form.

Once this research is completed, each student, separately, prepares two lists of descriptive words about the organization, under the headings "abstract" and "concrete." The separate lists are combined into two master lists, one for abstract and one for concrete characteristics.

The students then begin an intense visual search with no finished product in mind. They put on paper *all* the images they can think of and select the "good" ones, for further development.

They may go through hundreds of sketches before they are ready to defend particular possibilities. Several directions may be chosen and pursued.

They reach a point where they feel strongly about one or a small number of ideas. Cute, trendy concepts go out the window.

165

Eventually they choose a single idea and begin to refine it, applying precise craftsmanship and great care concerning form, counterform, weight, proportion, and so on.

While they develop the symbol, they also design the organization's logotype.

The students next apply the symbol in many situations and sizes, on several promotion pieces, testing the design in action to see if it retains high recognition value in varied use.

Their previous studies of letterforms bear fruit in this assignment, especially their work on form and counterform.

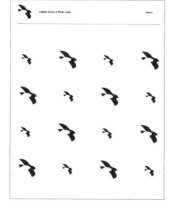

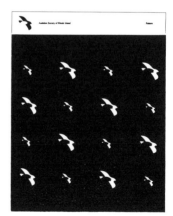

Save the Bay

Save the Bay was organized to restore
and protect the Narragansett Bay and its
watershed.

Tools for Training

A nonprofit grass roots organization that accepts tools from manufacturers and others to send to schools in underdeveloped countries.

international institute of rhode island

International Institute of Rhode Island

This agency helps immigrants in Southeastern New England become self-reliant, productive members of society and improves awareness and understanding of the cultural heritage and traditions that these newcomers bring to the United States.

Graphic Standards Manual

An assignment to write, design, and produce a simple publication, a "Graphic Standards Manual," that describes the origin and application of the symbol and logotype the students designed for the previous assignment.

In this manual, they explain the reasoning behind their design; they also give instructions on how the symbol is to be used by others.

This exercise forces the students to reexamine their design and its envisioned use. In many cases, reconsideration prompts them to revise the original, "final" version.

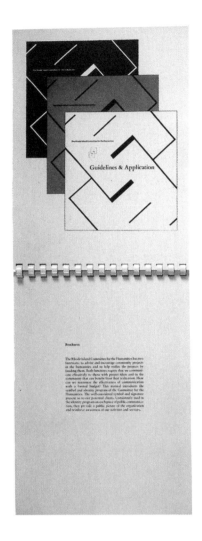

Design Application

For this project the students write and design an 8 1/2″ × 11″ brochure, in three sections, about a man-made object. The first section states the object's significance; the second covers historical or background information; the third shows how the object functions.

The process we follow is similar to that described in the section on "Form and Structure," which occurs earlier in this book. That section focuses on formal aspects of design; this one attempts to simulate the sort of problem solving demanded by "real life" situations. School is a hothouse environment. We try to give a taste of the world of professional practice. Only a taste is possible. There is no way to expose students to the real thing, its sorrows or its pleasures.

Designers are usually given jobs that are tightly constrained; the purposes are explicit; materials are specified; the audience is closely defined. Seldom are there wide degrees of freedom. We want students to work inventively within such constraints—and produce work that appeals to non-designers. We are not designing for each other. This assignment makes that point. You have to target the audience and hit it. Or fail.

If we accept the notion that good design is a fusion of art and craft, a designer must rise above limitations, or exploit them, making a virtue of necessity, making the ordinary extraordinary.

Each section of the class is given its own object, a bicycle, an abacus, whatever.

This kind of practical assignment helps students apply what they have learned in earlier assignments. Practice is as necessary for a designer as it is for a musician. Talent is never enough.

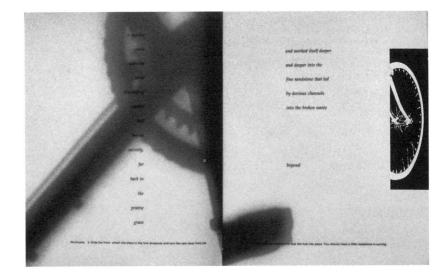

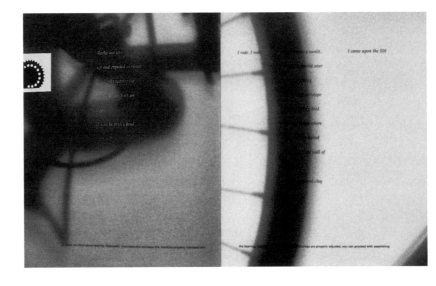

Part of a piece promoting bicycles.

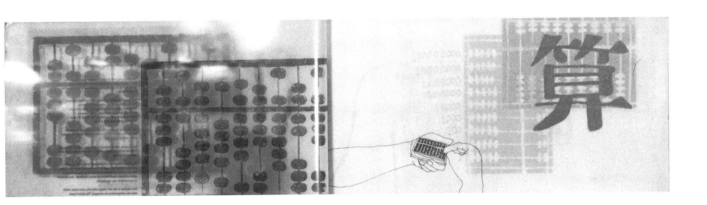

The abacus, a calculating device still used in Asia, has a frame divided into upper and lower portions set with moveable beads on parallel rods. It is a simple, elegant device whose structure lends itself to exciting design.

This assignment can be approached from a cultural, historical, or technological point of view. There are lots of ways to consider this ancient mechanism; it has an intriguing shape, an inherently interesting design in its own right. And its function is rich with meaning.

This assignment is based on engraved Peruvian gourds, a craft dating back more than 2,500 years. The wonderfully intricate decorations illustrate cultural events: processions, bullfights, folk dances, important personages, and ancient myths.

One reason why I give this assignment is that reference material on decorated gourds is scarce. The students must dig deep to find information. Another reason: It gives them the pleasure of surprise in discovering the cultural and artistic significance of this humble object.

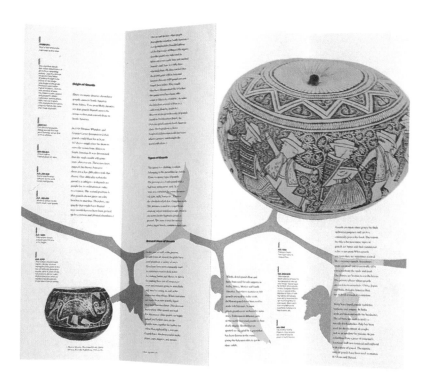

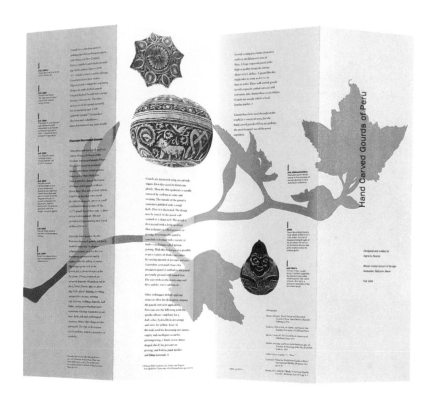

Professional Practice

From School to Studio

Efforts to solve the preceding exercises help students develop strategies for solving problems in the world beyond school. If one wants to learn one kind of operation, using one style and one technique, these projects will not suit the purpose.

I have heard it argued that there is little room for self expression in graphic design. Not so. But the designer does have to be involved in the work at hand, aesthetically, emotionally, and intellectually, in order to find room for self expression.

Designers are routinely caught in the tension between freedom and constraint. Students must learn to balance creative liberty and practical limitations. A tricky business. But striking that balance is very much the essence of the enterprise.

The next section contains examples from my professional practice. In most cases, I include captions that give some background or explain intentions.

Discussing a metal typeface in Noel Martin's 1957 typography class at the Art Academy of Cincinnati. *Front right,* Malcolm Grear.

From Student to Professional

Most design firms, when hiring recent graduates, look for people who are enthusiastic, serious, confident, creative. The best firms look for visual and conceptual skills. They want someone who will take risks; they prefer candidates with backgrounds in design and liberal arts, with a foundation in drawing, three-dimensional studies, photography, and computer composition and graphics. It helps if one knows the history of graphic design and can speak and write clearly. Such skills are needed when making presentations or directing others. Also, explaining a design often clarifies one's ideas and leads to improvements in the design itself. The designer works within a complex web of social, economic, scientific, and technological forces. The more you know, the better.

First and foremost, one needs aesthetic sensibility. Design is a form of art. If it is approached as art, a certain dignity can be sustained to help ward off the venalities of the marketplace.

For our studio we seek colleagues with agile minds, a sense of humor, a positive outlook, who enjoy working with others. When interviewing a prospective colleague, I often learn more from the conversation than the portfolio. Pieces in a portfolio can say more about the teacher than the student who created them. If a teacher has not given a student ample opportunity to express talents in an independent manner, an impressive portfolio can mask a lack of maturity and creative reserves essential to meet new and surprising challenges. Such teaching may seem effective in the short term—handsome works may be produced—but the student risks facing painful realities down the road. Under the press of deadlines and the demands of clients and co-workers, a newcomer in professional practice may sorely miss the basic training in resilience, good humor, fundamental skills, and necessary confidence that a more realistic education would have instilled.

A design meeting at Malcolm Grear Designers.

Design as a Business

I am often asked how to start a design business. Starting is simple; continuing takes strong commitment.

What is now Malcolm Grear Designers began in 1960 in the basement of a small apartment. I worked at a desk near the furnace. In our next apartment, I set up shop in the attic. Soon the traffic up and down stairs (clients, typesetters, printing salesmen, paper merchants) became so heavy that my family lost all privacy. I had to find a studio away from the house.

My first design job came by way of a jazz musician who recommended me to a classical musician who owned a piano store. My task was to design a symbol. This project brought in two more, which brought in four, then eight. And so it goes.

The number of people working in our studio grew with each move, from one to two, to five, to twelve. I am careful not to let it get larger than a dozen. This seems to be the optimum number for us. It is more difficult to remain this size than to get larger.

Our group grew in number because the jobs got bigger, not more numerous. A staff of twelve is large enough to handle almost any project and not so large that we can't afford to accept small jobs.

It is a heady thought to realize that many people reading this book will have come across something designed by Malcolm Grear Designers—a sign, part of a corporate identity program, college textbook, trade book, brochure, exhibit, art book, museum catalogue, or poster. There is some satisfaction in seeing the results of the work in the outside world. But for me the main pleasure is the work itself.

In this piece, Varujan Boghosian, a sculptor,
did me the honor of altering my work, including stone blocks and wooden bird, thereby
converting my art into "our" art.

182

Design Commissions

Work on a new job begins when we receive an invitation to submit a proposal. The invitation usually gives a reasonably full account of the design problem that we must address.

We begin proposals with a description of the project as we see it and we follow with a list of phases that we think will lead to a satisfying conclusion.

I am making this process seem bloodless, a perfunctory routine that leads to quick agreement with the client. Reality, of course, is sharply different. We live in a competitive world. Other designers or architects may be contending for the same job. So as you read the steps we take, please imagine a studio galvanized to win the day. There is tension, spirit, and determination in these efforts to close the deal—an essential and demanding part of the business.

Our first phase is research and analysis. We need to discover what the design must accomplish. The depth of research is determined by the complexity of the project.

For large, complicated projects, the second phase involves preparation and presentation of design ideas in considerable detail. Clear communication between client and designer at this point can save hours of ill-conceived effort. If we have misunderstood the client's circumstance and purposes, discussions during presentation can put us back on track.

In phase three we present a "final" concept, which includes all aspects of the project. The previous phase and this one are normally the most time-consuming; they are also the most energized, creative, and exciting. Preparing presentations may require hundreds of sketches. It's great fun—sometimes.

In the fourth phase we revise and refine the design; in the fifth, we complete finished art for printing or, if the project is architectural, we generate drawings to guide fabrication.

Phase six, supervision of production, is our chance to make sure we get the product that we want. Then we send a bill—a happy phase seven!

The time and fee schedule, which may cover weeks or years, is, of course, an important element in the initial proposal.

All projects require some sort of proposal, although many are of modest size and don't require elaborate presentations.

For new clients, a proposal allows them to evaluate the designer's ideas and skills. For the designer, preparing and presenting the proposal can help shake out the chaff, reducing the project to essentials.

This whole process of devising, presenting, discussing, and revising a proposal is a necessary mechanism for communication between a client and designer who do not know each other. Once a working relationship is established between client and designer it is unlikely that the client will need ornate proposals on future projects. A brief account of design ideas will probably suffice.

Counterform/Form

In these three examples, black letter-forms generate counterforms.

The white letters provide a focal point, giving the symbol visual life, as they move in and out of focus with a blink of the eye.

Symbol 1967
Mount Holyoke College

The M is the dominant element; the H emerges.

A Symbol Study 1980
The Department of Health and Human Services

You see the two H's before you notice the S.

Symbol 1962
Color Concentrate Corporation

A symbol for the industry, not intended for the general public.

Color concentrates are pulverized between three rollers. The inside white form is the strongest and is noticed before the C's.

Symbol 1992
Manomet Observatory

Interface between sea and land. The interdependency of drawn elements, form and counterform, represents the interaction of wildlife populations and natural systems.

Posters 1969
The Solomon R. Guggenheim Museum

An example where white is the form, symbolizing the museum, and the darker color is
counterform.

We wanted a poster that conveyed the symbolic power of this monumental building while
remaining a viable piece of art on its own.

These one-color posters serve a dual purpose. They are sold in the museum shop as independent works; they are also used to promote events, by overprinting messages in the white area.

The shapes were drawn and redrawn many times to achieve the right curves, the planar quality, and the interaction between form and counterform.

If the outline of the building had simply been traced from a photograph, the poster would have seemed flat and inactive, failing to capture the rhythmic form of Frank Lloyd Wright's building.

The poster is printed from one printing plate with only one color on each poster, requiring a change of ink for each color.

Production costs were kept to a minimum. We did this design in 1969; the poster has been reprinted many times since then, raising a lot of money for the museum. I have seen them hanging on walls throughout the world.

Architecture
and the
Incomplete City

ACSA Northeast Regional Meeting

October 3, 4, 1985

The physical structure of
the late twentieth century
American city is indetermi-
nate, open-ended, often con-
tradictory, and specifically
incomplete. As the site of
speculation and laissez-faire
development, the aesthetic
force of this city resists the
designer's traditional efforts
toward harmony, order and
completion. The distinctions
between the images of
high culture and popular
commerce, the hierarchy
between planned urban
centers and the periphery
of disrespectful objects, have
been erased. Consequently
this city refuses analysis or
synthesis in terms of the
architectural canons of the
European capitals.

This symposium seeks to
engage discussion and
debate on this condition in
the following areas:

• Emerging typologies
in design: The critical
reformulation, reinterpre-
tation or architecturali-
zation of the commercial
organisms of the capitalist
city. (See Rodolfo Machado,
"Domains of Architecture,"
New Art Examiner, vol. 10,
No. 9 (June 1983) p. 9)

• Historical analysis: Address-
ing the historiographical
vacuum of documentation
and analytic methods of the
twentieth century American
city.

• The role of architecture:
Can the present condition of
this city provide conceptual
and aesthetic models for a
new architecture? Can the
architectural object acquire
renewed symbolic power?
Can architecture resist
economic optimization?

Charles Sheeler, New York, 1920
The Museum of Fine Arts, Houston, Museum Purchase

Call For Papers

A one page, single-spaced
abstract should be submitted
to the organizers of the symposium at the address below
not later than July 1, 1985.
The format of typed papers
will be forwarded on acceptance of the abstract. The
organizers will undertake to
publish accepted papers.

Professors
Michael Hays, George Wagner
ACSA 1985 N.E. Regional Meeting
Department of Architecture
Rhode Island School of Design
2 College Street
Providence, RI 02903

Department of Architecture

Rhode Island School of Design

Providence, Rhode Island

Poster 1985
Department of Architecture
Rhode Island School of Design

A poster that served as an invitation to submit papers for a conference on *Architecture and the Incomplete City*.

We chose this photograph of New York by Charles Sheeler, 1920, as the dominant image because the buildings and empty spaces and the light and shadows suit the topics: *Emerging Typologies in Design, Historical Analysis,* and *The Role of Architecture in the City.*

The flatness of the small orange square and the typography create another dimension within the poster, setting up tension between the two and three dimensional planes. The squares also show a fragmented grid pattern, resonating with main topics in the text.

Line, Weight, and Dimension

Varying the width of a line can give an
illusion of volume and a kind of
pulsating motion as the eye moves back
and forth from one plane to another.

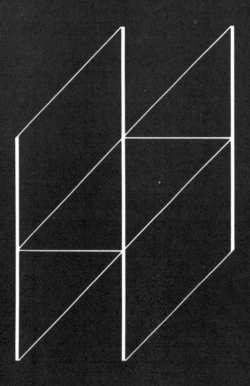

Symbol 1962
Howell Design Associates

A company involved with interior spaces.

To suggest space while also suggesting such
objects as shelves, containers, furniture, and
so on.

Symbol 1968
National Bickford/Foremost

Symbol for a company that markets color separations and printing. National Bickford (color separators) joined forces with Foremost Lithographers.

The change in perspective makes the image oscillate.

The symbol suggests multiple aspects of the business: Color separations are scanned on a cylinder; offset printing is done on three rollers; both companies produce images on paper.

Symbol 1972
Brier Manufacturing Company

This symbol, which wraps around and enters
and exits itself, is analogous to an ingenious
machine that the company devised to place
semi-precious stones on jewelry items.

The varied line weights generate a sense of
activity and volume.

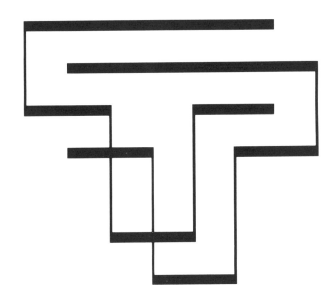

Symbol 1983
Twins Foundation

About identical twins.
Two identical letterforms, each tightly related
to the other.

Visual Switch

A pulsing movement: At one time, one part appears to be forward; at another, the other.

194

Symbol 1963
Brown University Press

To convey the spirit of a university that publishes conflicting views: popular and unpopular, fact and fiction, science and religion, unresolved research and established knowledge.

The diagonal lines cause the virtual planes to switch back and forth.

This dynamic quality lifts the symbol above the paper, keeping it dominant even when surroundings are visually competitive.

Symbol 1965
Bay State Abrasives

A company that manufactures grinding
wheels and other abrasives.

The use of black and white and the change
of perspective induce a sense of action.

Symbol 1978
NEPTCO

The symbol was originally designed for New England Printed Tape, a company that manufactured and printed ribbon for gift wrapping.

The company has since changed its name and product. It uses the same equipment to manufacture insulating and conductive tapes for the computer industry. The same symbol is used with the new name, a change that would have required a new symbol if this one had been strictly literal.

The switching of planes adds interest to the image, making it dynamic.

Light and Tension

The interaction of lines of varying
weight and color creates a glowing effect
within the composition.

Symbol 1979
Sonesta International Hotels

An international chain of hotels.
The goal: to convey a global feeling,
without being too literal.

Symbol 1961
Short Line, Inc.

A bus company that makes short trips.

The two arrows suggest a continual coming and going.

The intent behind the symbol is to show that the bus will not drop you off and forget about you; it will return to take you back to your starting point.

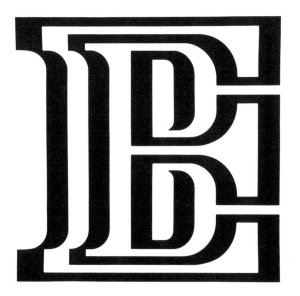

Symbol 1980
Banco de A. Edwards

The symbol for Banco de Edwards, a bank in
Chile. The symbol works bilingually; the
bank is known in other parts of the world as
Edwards Bank.

The "B" is dominant when you read Banco de
Edwards. The "E" is dominant when you read
Edwards Bank.

The power of the symbol suggests the power
of the enterprise.

auction
action
auction
action

Typographic Image for an Event 1969
Museum of Art
Rhode Island School of Design

The words need not be read in a particular order.

You get a multiple reading: action auction, auction action, action action, and so on. Meaning and image are dynamic.

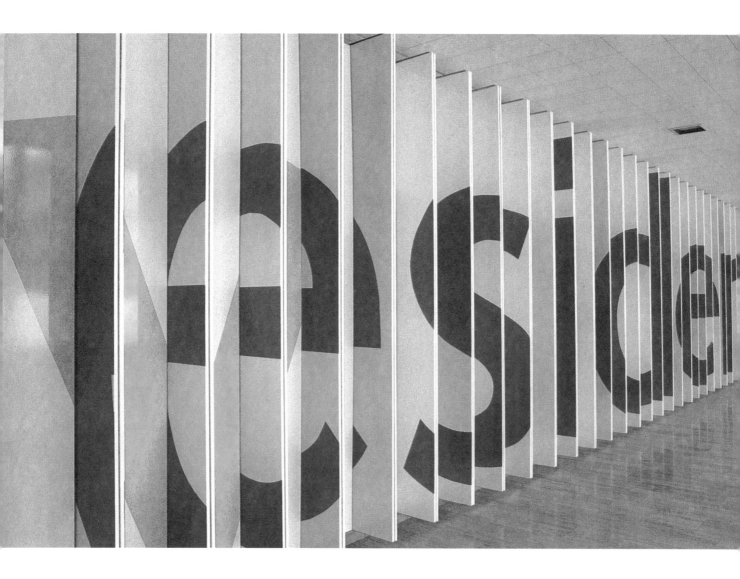

View from one direction.

Signs 1975
Hugh Stubbins/Rex Allen Partnership

Outpatient Department, School and
Residence, Boston City Hospital

A sign can do more than label a place or give
directions. In this case the architects wanted
to brighten up what they considered a dead
area by installing lively signs that also give
clear information.

These signs are not critical to the day-to-day
operations of the hospital; they are located in
a hallway that connects the educational section to the residences and are opposite a glass
wall overlooking a courtyard. If you look
straight at the sign from the courtyard, you
see "Gymnasium" (not shown in this shot).
The wall is alive with letterforms and counterforms, color and texture.

View from the other (same wall).

Symbol 1968
Sapphire Bay

A vacation resort in the Virgin Islands. The slo-
gan for the Virgin Islands is "Island in the Sun."
The resort is on the ocean. These two attributes are conveyed by arrangement of the S's.

Symbol 1981
Solar Cities and Towns

A program initiated by the Department of
Energy to provide models of energy
conservation and the use of solar energy
on an urban scale.

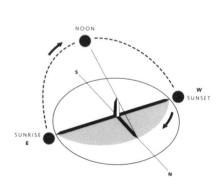

An impressionistic interpretation of a
diagram tracking the sun's path.

Symbol 1973
Roger Williams Foods

A wholesale distributor of foods.

The main idea is that the sun is the source of
all life on earth. Multiple symbols: sickle suggests harvesting; this form evolves to suggest
ladles and spoons—bringing the harvest to
table; the spiral-like form in the center suggests
a cornucopia—symbol of plenty. The closeness
and weight change of the lines suggest light
being released. Sunlight becomes food.

Expanded Meaning

Symbol 1962
Merrimack Valley Textile Museum

A museum on the history of textile technology and the industrial revolution.

The design suggests textile technology. The rhythm of lines and spaces gives an illusion of movement reminiscent of the Jacquard looms.

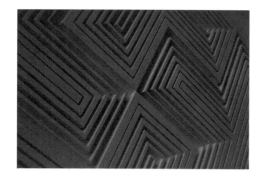

Symbol 1978
Danny Ferrington

A distinguished maker of musical instruments.
These instruments are sensitively built, perfect
in tone. The clef and the initial F evolved to
become synonymous.

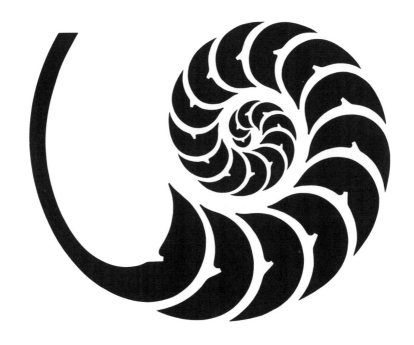

Symbol 1973
Cannon Partnership

A holding company that owns many other
companies, one of which is Cannon Design,
which in turn has many divisions.

A stylized nautilus, symbol for a company
with many parts or chambers, each an integral part of the whole. A line through the
nautilus shell connects each chamber, imply-
ing that each separate company in the
partnership is related to the others. The wide
end of the spiral suggests future growth.

Symbol 1979
Metropolitan Opera

Each M overlaps the counterform of the next
M, giving a build-up of color; the M's give
the illusion of dancing or spinning. The whole
composition forms the shape of an O, for Opera.

Humor in Design

Humor is a compelling form of human
communication, and designers use it
when the occasion allows.

Symbol and Promotional Materials 1989
Community Preparatory School

A school for gifted, underprivileged children,
fourth to eighth grade.

I wanted to convey life, energy, enthusiasm,
pleasure, and curiosity. I wanted to affect others the way I had been affected when I visited
the school—it made me happy.

Community
Preparatory
School

Symbol 1968
Morris Museum of Arts and Sciences

A museum mainly for children; it has an outstanding collection of puppets.

The two M's form a puppet-like composition with head, feet, and hands missing. The children are invited to draw whatever kinds of heads, hands, and feet they like. For promotional purposes, head, feet, and hands can be added to the symbol.

In the late nineteenth century, the Presbyterian Church split into three parts; each had its own symbol.

In 1958, two of these sections joined to form the United Presbyterian Church in the USA.

In 1983, after 122 years of separation, dating from the Civil War, the remaining division joined the others to form the Presbyterian Church (USA).

At this time, a committee was formed to bring to the Presbyterian General Assembly an official seal and symbol. The committee of nine members comprised people from both sides. Even though the sections had joined in principle, there were still differences to be ironed out.

It became obvious—after a contest had been sponsored and six hundred entries submitted—that the design of this symbol was more complicated than had been imagined.

The Committee wanted a symbol whose qualities would not be exhausted at first glance. They rejected mottos—especially Latin. They felt that the new symbol should be more formal than informal and that it should have a strong structure.

Forty-six designers throughout the United States were invited to submit their credentials. That number was trimmed to ten, then to three. The Committee visited each of the three firms for further interviews. Our firm was selected.

We were thrilled. This project had deep significance for everyone involved with the Church—ministers, elders, and lay members alike. And it mattered a lot to us.

When the Committee accepted our design, they recommended to a forty-member board that I make a presentation to the General Assembly (2,500 people). I was told that in the entire history of the Presbyterian General Assembly that there had only been one unanimous vote.

If the General Assembly showed approval, it would go to the forty-member board and then to a seven hundred-member Governing Board, which would determine final acceptance or rejection.

This struck me as a bit too democratic. I had grandly stated on many occasions that I would not play to a cast of thousands when seeking approval of our designs. But I was in this race to stay.

The symbol for the Presbyterian Church (USA) was one of the most coveted design commissions to come along in years. From my viewpoint, it headed the list of challenges, not because of religious belief but because of the symbolic power inherent in the Church. There is an aura of mystery about this ancient institution that fascinates me. I also felt that corporations had "out-symbolized" the Church.

Once we were awarded the contract, we were told that the new symbol must include four components: fire, the cross, a descending dove, and the book.

I did hundreds of sketches, but could not move beyond pictorial images of a bird and a book. I came down hard on myself, fearing that I was losing my zip. I worked on possibilities all day every day and most of every night. I dreamed about the symbol during whatever time was left for sleep.

When at last I got what I felt was right, I made a tall hat with the symbol on it and paraded through the studio to cheers, whistles, and manic applause. This was at two o'clock in the morning! My colleagues were greatly relieved to see the crisis pass, the curtain rise on brighter times.

At my presentation to the General Assembly, I said, "I suppose it's much like a good sermon. You feel it when you have it." A lone voice in the audience said, "Amen." This scared the hell out of me. The symbol was accepted by unanimous vote of all sections. They gave me a fifteen minute standing ovation. Heady stuff!

The Cross

The Dove

The Fish

The Book

The Pulpit

The Cup

The Fire

The Triangle

Seal and Symbol 1985
Presbyterian Church (USA)

The new symbol communicates to people of
all backgrounds and ages. It is easily seen,
recognized, and interpreted.

The symbol is used in diverse ways—vestments, etched glass, and, in collaboration with artist Ed McIlvane, two stained glass windows 19 feet in height.

The "seal" reflects the union of two churches that share a common mission. It acknowledges the past by incorporating the symbols important to both churches prior to their union, thus reflecting the traditions that have come together to form the new Presbyterian Church (USA).

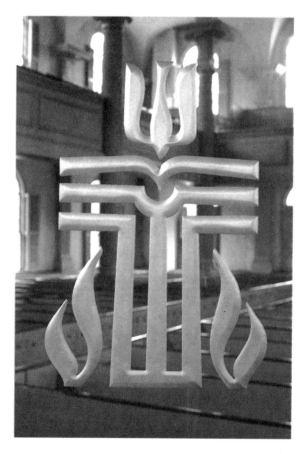

When we have completed the design of a visual identity program, we devise a manual that shows the client how to employ the design in various ways. This manual of design standards is a prime working tool for communicating guidelines efficiently and economically. It is the end product of the design process and insures against ineffectual use of the design. The manual governs the use of the design plan in all applications, thereby clarifying and simplifying communications between designer and client.

If applied in a haphazard, unsupervised manner, the design can be distorted and weakened, its power dissipated. While the manual limits the ways in which some things can be done, it helps maintain the design.

Considerable research must be done to prepare the manual. Hours are spent in meetings. The client's existing materials are examined and their functions reviewed. For one client, we stopped counting when we reached 300 different sizes of paper used by the organization prior to our new design. We trimmed the sizes down to four. Every single application must be dealt with separately, each must be produced in finished form and photographed for inclusion in the manual.

Once the manual is ready, we usually conduct training sessions to show the client how best to use the design in a wide array of applications.

A study of printed materials shows sizes of paper used prior to our involvement.

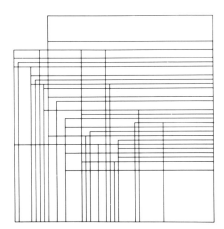

Recommended sizes of paper.

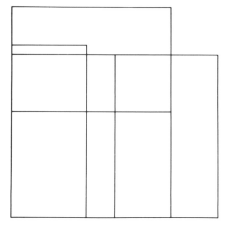

Pages from a Manual 1981
United States Navy

Non-Repetitive Identity

In a "repetitive" identity program, the placement of all design elements is highly constrained and rigorously consistent. For example, the symbol is always in precisely the same places, controlled by the rules specified explicitly in the design plan. In a "non-repetitive" identity program, no formula or exact system is followed, although there is a strong visual relationship from one application to the other.

Visual Identity 1969
The Solomon R. Guggenheim Museum

How can you miss when you are working with the strong, energetic lines of Frank Lloyd Wright's powerful form—almost any curve or circle fits into the visual family.

A consistent, repeated format is sometimes an effective system for certain periodicals or series publications, such as the Calendar of Events.

A book bag is a walking billboard, not just an attractive wrapper.

Poster 1968
Dartmouth College

The actual piece of art shown in this poster
for Varujan Boghosian and Dartmouth College
is recessed in a box-like container. The edges
of the poster represent the container. The
outstretched arms invite the viewer into the
poster and into the exhibition.

The poster is printed by silkscreen in white
and black on tan paper. The limited amount of
color typifies Boghosian's work: strong form
with a subtle use of color.

The type is arranged to appear centered,
although it is not — an example of visual rather
than mathematical accuracy. If it were centered exactly, it would appear awkward.

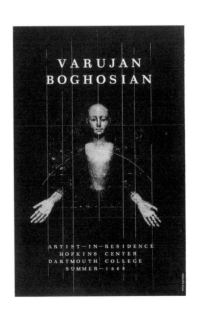

VARUJAN
BOGHOSIAN

ARTIST—IN—RESIDENCE
HOPKINS CENTER
DARTMOUTH COLLEGE
SUMMER—1968

Signs Without Words

Environmental Design 1972
Oakwood Comprehensive Training Center

The forms on top of the poles respond to the
shape of the banners hanging below.

In contrast to most mental health facilities, where patients are contained by walls or fences, Oakwood was built to be open and residential, with each house serving twelve children and their counselor. Children are encouraged to stay, without coercion or force.

The surrounding community approved, but no one wanted Oakwood next door. During construction, Oakwood was referred to as an insane asylum, and petitions demanded fences.

The facility was nearly completed, with children already resident, when we were asked to design signage and other elements that would give visual vitality to the architecture, which many in the community felt was sombre and imposing. We wanted to change the community's view, to show that Oakwood is a safe and desirable place. The majority of the children at Oakwood would be coming from Kentucky's mountains and farming sections. Moving would be a major adjustment for them. We incorporated familiar things—native materials, bird houses. Logs from the mountains were debarked by hand axes and used in play structures. Discarded tractor seats were sandblasted and painted to become outside seating. Concrete culvert pipes were turned vertically and filled with dirt to become vegetable gardens.

Painted concrete pipes to crawl through.

Sculpture by Hugh Townley becomes an entrance sign.

Sculpture by Ed Koren.

Very little effort was required to convince sculptor Hugh Townley and cartoonist Ed Koren, both well-known artists, to join our effort. Hugh produced a large sculpture composed of three parts. Persuading state officials that the sculpture could be the main entrance sign was no easy chore. Some community officials felt that the sculpture was too abstract; they feared that no one would understand it.

As the sculpture was being installed by workmen who were mainly from the mountains, one of them asked me, "Mr. Grear, what does it mean?" I asked, "What does it mean to you?" He stepped back, looked up at the sculpture, and said, "Well, it's like a piece of music. If you put the right notes together it makes a pretty sound." I don't think I could have done as well.

Ed Koren prepared small drawings that we enlarged and had cut from several layers of wood; these were laminated by Hugh Townley. Then Ed painted the wood. The children and their counselor gave those creatures names.

Some of the children were so mentally or physically disabled that they were confined to bed. To draw their eyes skyward, we designed bird houses for martins and placed these outside their windows. Martins are recognized and revered by Kentuckians.

I designed a sculpture and placed it on top of a pole. It turns slowly with even a slight wind. The piece was built by a local welder, who thought that he was making a fancy antenna.

We designed banners and flags with poles and supports shaped to suggest banners. The poles remain visually active even when the banners are missing. The children continue to make banners from the patterns we supplied.

The patterns on draperies throughout the Oakwood Center are based on letter forms. These were made by inmates of a Kentucky prison as part of their industrial program; they were taught to silkscreen fabric. We also created sculptured forms on which the children could perfect their balancing skills. And we painted patterns on paved areas, where the children could skip and jump.

For the nonambulatory section we installed terrariums to be maintained by ambulatory patients. The plants and creatures were taken from a small swamp on the property; we drew attention to the swamp by erecting tall, brightly colored poles among the reeds, bushes, stumps, and dead trees.

We had some trouble encouraging the state bureaucracy to plant five acres of wild flowers—they thought of them as weeds—but they acquiesced.

The sculptured entrance by Hugh Townley has since become an important symbol for the whole community, almost like a bell tower. Its outlines are now used, in relief, on plaques that the Chamber of Commerce distributes, and the shapes, drawn in silhouette, have been used in the local newspaper. The sculpture signifies more than the Center itself; it now stands for the surrounding community. In a touching description, the children wrote that "the umbrella shape means sheltering; the circular shapes mean rings of hope; the cutout heart means love."

If we had yielded to the bureaucracy, the sculpture would not be there. In its place, a large sign would proclaim that place to be the Comprehensive Training Center for Mentally Disturbed Children. Those Kentucky prisoners would not have learned the craft and pleasure of silkscreen printing.

Birdhouses for martins.

Wind sculpture.

Sculptural forms to walk on.

Drapery patterns based on letterforms.

Sculpture by Ed Koren.

Function Following Form

We were asked to design and produce a memento to be distributed at a ceremony dedicating a new city being built from scratch in Saudi Arabia.

With no particular idea in mind, I began by folding up the corners of a square piece of paper; as the folding continued, the paper took on the form of an empty cube. I liked the container, wanted to use it, but then had to decide what kind of memento could be devised to fit inside it. Here we were clearly breaking the rule about form following function. The container came before the contents!

We had previously designed, as part of this same project, three bronze plates for a monument designed by Spero Daltas, an architect in Rome. These plates had been placed on the top surfaces of a one meter cube of granite, which had been installed sitting on one of its corners.

We decided that a further interpretation of Spero's monument would be appropriate for this commission.

The memento was designed as a cube with four-inch sides. We used leather for the container; the cube was made from the same kind of granite that had been used for the dedication monument. The metal plates applied to the three top sides are a reduction of the artwork previously prepared. The plates are made of brass as is the triangular base, which neatly fits against the little cube when the whole memento is snugly in its leather wrapper.

The leather case was made in New York; the base and engraved plates in Providence. The stone was cut in Rome by the same stone carver who had cut the original monument. The cases, bases and plates were then sent to Rome where the complete package was assembled.

In the design business, as in others, one does whatever it takes to finish the job on time. Three weeks from the initiation of this project, one hundred of these awards were distributed at the dedication ceremony.

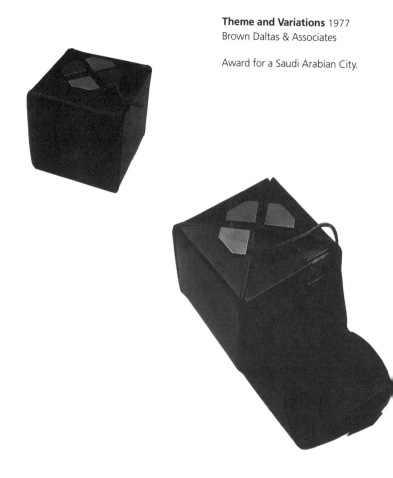

Theme and Variations 1977
Brown Daltas & Associates

Award for a Saudi Arabian City.

City Plan.

The project began with the design of a book
to be given to King Khalid of Saudi Arabia.

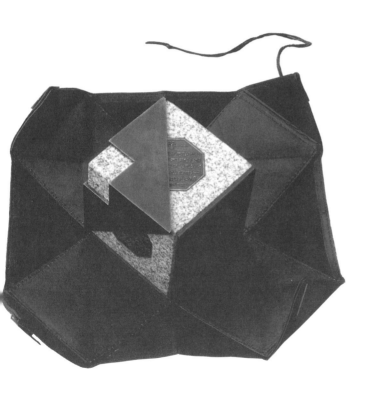
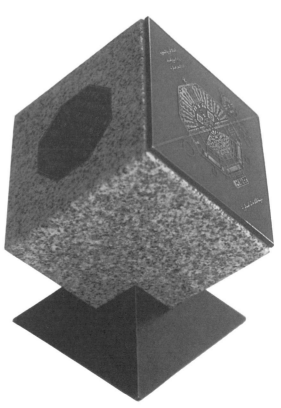

Time, Space, and Position

The old Majestic Theatre in Providence became the new home of the Trinity Repertory Theatre. Painted signs covered the brick facade. We added two huge masks made of wire mesh, classic symbols of drama in a new form, another layer of visual assertion placed against and fusing with the earlier layers.

A member of Trinity Theatre's promotional staff had the bright idea of attaching to each wire visage a big red plastic bag, stuffed full, to advertise a production of the play *Red Noses*.

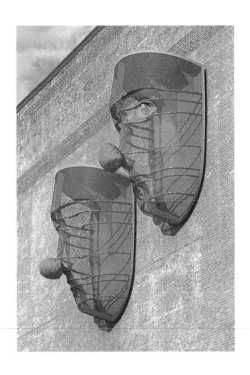

Combining Old and New 1981
Trinity Repertory Theatre

The masks take on a different character and facial expression as lighting conditions change, from winter to summer, morning to evening, bright to overcast, and as the viewer changes position in relation to them. This continual change stirs the imagination, represents the flux of human circumstance, and captures the spirit of a highly inventive theatrical enterprise.

We got the idea from an antique wire mask popular at Mardi Gras celebrations. Another source was the scenes painted on screen-like material in the back windows of trucks and vans.

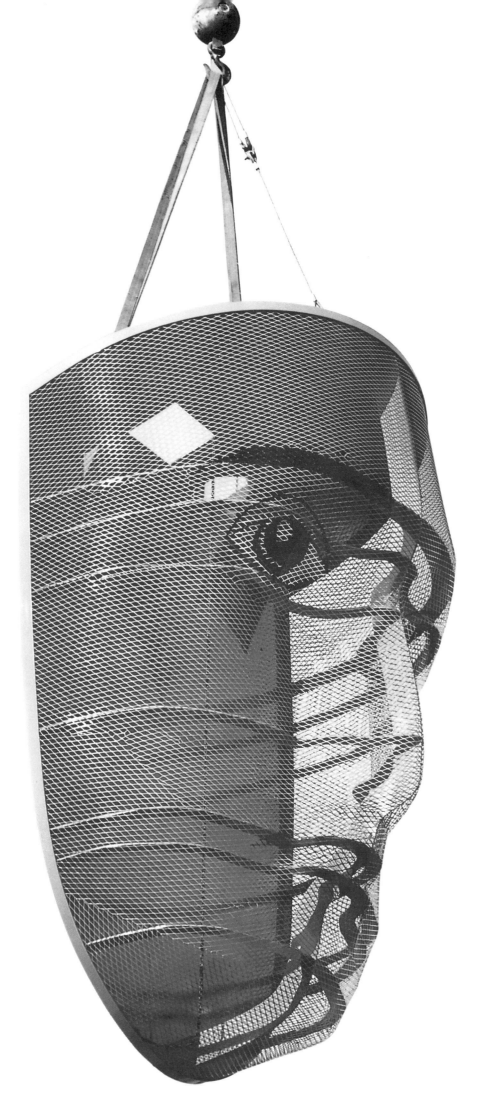

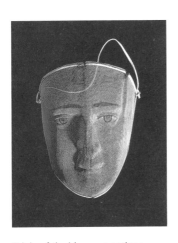

Origin of the idea — an antique wire mask.

Scale Relationship

Announcement 1979
The Providence Art Club

A natural scale relation.

No frills or fancy stuff for this low-budget announcement of a three-person exhibition.

Works by the three artists were illustrated in a single photograph. Posters that I had previously designed for the other two artists represented my work; the illustrations within the posters showed pieces by Dale Chihuly and Hugh Townley.

I used a serving table to hold a piece of Dale's glass, giving the composition a strong horizontal axis.

I grandly added silhouettes of our ambitious faces to the regimented alignment of famous faces placed around the club's walls. Our three mugs are at the extreme right.

Dale Chihuly
Malcolm Grear
Hugh Townley

Closing Party
Friday, January 19, 1979, 5 - 8 pm
The Providence Art Club
11 Thomas Street

Poster 1972
Brown University

We define scale by showing the artist standing next to his work. The enlarged section of the sculpture reveals the bold texture of the materials.

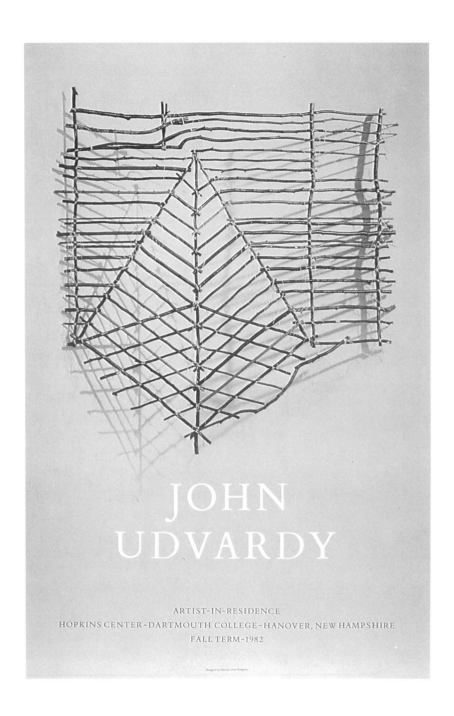

Poster 1982
Dartmouth College

If John Udvardy's sculpture were photographed straight on, it would lack depth. Instead, the sculpture was photographed across the corner of a wall. The shadows draw attention to the 3/D character of the sculpture.

The subtle background color gives a warm contrast for the sculpture and a nice home for the artist's name.

Sign 1981
Museum of Fine Arts, Boston, and
I. M. Pei & Partners

The letters were carved, off center, in a course
of stone to catch the light. We took into
account the shadow from the overhanging
entrance.

Interior and Exterior Signs 1981
Museum of Fine Arts, Boston,
and I.M. Pei & Partners

These signs are quiet, restrained, but suitably
informative.

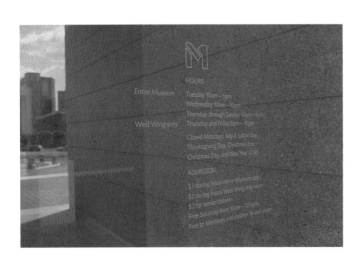

Signs

For three-dimensional projects, including exhibits and signs, we construct models of the design elements for which we are responsible.

Often at the initiation of these projects, the related buildings and landscape exist only on paper as architectural plans. If so, we also construct models of the buildings and other dominant elements in the immediate neighborhood.

A sign system, generally identifying, directing, and informing, must function on two levels. It guides the first-time or infrequent visitor, whose initial confusion must be promptly allayed. The system must also function on a second, more subtle level, fulfilling the needs of those whose lives are centered on this environment for months or years. As people come and go on a daily basis, the graphic elements ought to provide a coherent visual system that communicates information clearly while enhancing the visual mood of the place. The sign system should be in harmony with the architecture, remaining distinctive but not aggressively imposing.

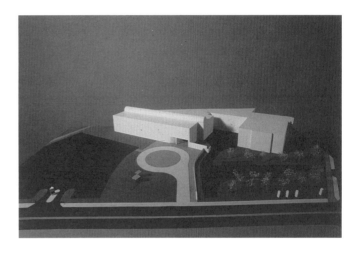

We went to some pains to make scale models of Pei's building and our proposed exterior signs to show their impact when placed at the perimeter of the architectural site.

Interior scale model: a light tube illuminates signs etched in glass.

Interior Signs 1985
Foremost Lithograph

Pictorial signs add visual energy by explicitly
showing activities the signs are intended to
identify.

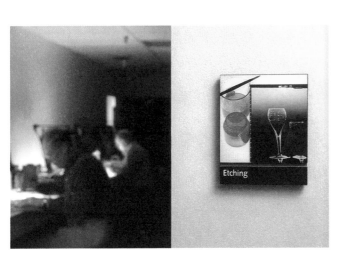

Identification Sign 1972
Roitman & Son, Inc.

This sign fits strongly into its environment,
including the building in the background, which
is next door to the furniture store that the
sign is identifying.

Directional Sign 1972
Big Canoe

This sign is for a housing project in the mountains.

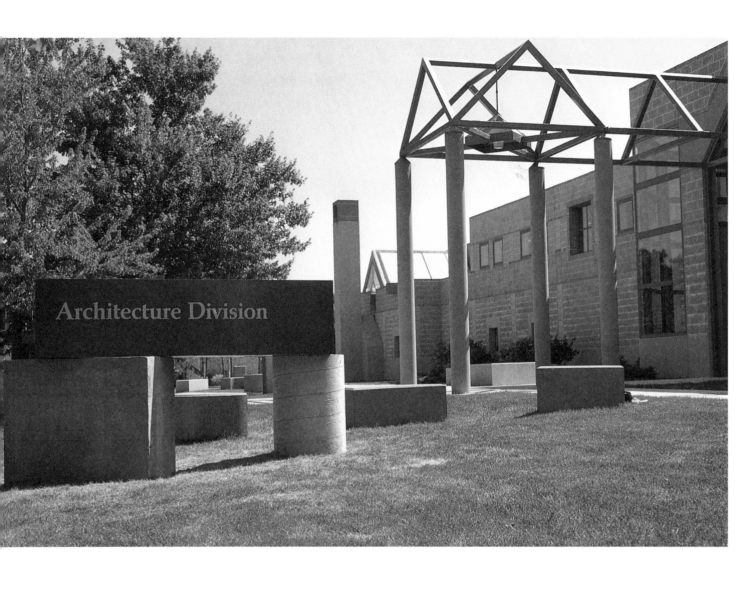

Interior and Exterior Signs 1985
Architecture Division
Roger Williams College

The design of the seats and the supports for
the sign suggest a child's building blocks.

Balance

The type on a poster announcing an exhibit of an artist's work must not overpower or compete with the image but must be strong enough to hold its own. No single typeface is suited to all kinds of art. The type and spacing must be in visual balance with the image.

People buy posters at museums because of the art that is on them, but few buy a reproduction if there are no words. I suppose a reproduction seems slightly fake, and a poster is frankly just what it is, without pretension.

Posters serve an important role in asserting the purpose of our museums. The image must be printed as accurately as possible, especially since this is as close as many will come to seeing the real thing.

Exhibition Poster 1971
The Solomon R. Guggenheim Museum

Exhibition Poster 1984
The Solomon R. Guggenheim Museum

Exhibition Poster 1978
The Solomon R. Guggenheim Museum

Performance Posters 1972
The Solomon R. Guggenheim Museum

These posters promote theatrical performances, thus allowing a different interaction between type and image than posters promoting exhibits.

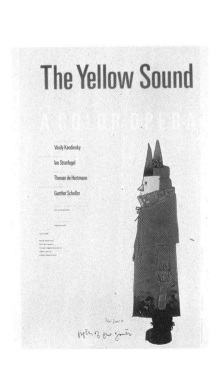

Exhibition Poster 1975
Dale Chihuly

The angle of the captions creates a rhythm
secondary to the one formed by horizontal
structure of the images.

Anniversary Poster 1978
Francis and Virgil Simpson

An evocation of time together, celebrating a
half century of marriage.

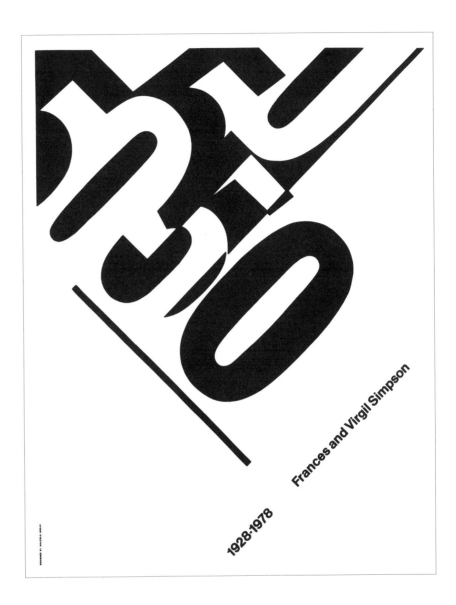

Black and White

There seems to be an infinite number of blacks. Beyond being warm or cold, black can have a velvet-like surface or a slick, shiny one; it can be deep or shallow.

When black and white are used in the right proportion and properly printed they convey astonishing elegance and drama. They take on color.

It may often seem that the easiest way to give an image muscle is to run it in abundant color, but that color, when used excessively, can exhaust the viewer's sensitivity and cripple the message.

Brochure 1978
Mohawk Paper Mills

Section from a brochure showing the "color" of black and white printing.

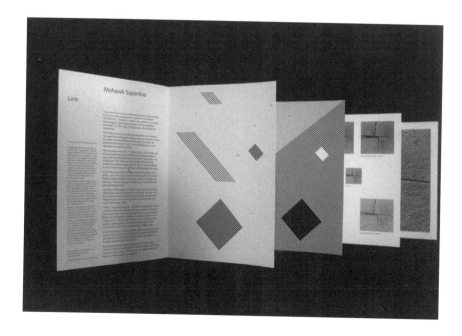

Catalogue Cover and Poster 1967
National Gallery of Art and The Museum of Art,
Rhode Island School of Design

Silkscreen: white on black.

When you open the double-page spread, the
images spring to life.

Theatre at the University of Rhode
Island is taught and practiced in a
growing and ambitious new department. After a long history of energetic
undergraduate involvement in the
University Theatre on the extra-
curricular level, a B.A. program in
Theatre was established in 1957. In
1966 the B.F.A. was added, and the
following year Theatre was established as a separate department with
a rapidly growing faculty, all of whose
members combine academic and
professional training.

The Department of Theatre provides
its majors the opportunity for involvement and training on several levels,
offering the Bachelor of Fine Arts degree in theatre for those whose career
goals are in the professional theatre.
The students in this program are
screened through interviews and au-
dition on the basis of talent and
potential. They are then given the
opportunity for artistic development
through a four-year curriculum of
carefully integrated studio and traditional academic class experiences.
Programs are offered in acting,
directing, and theatre design and
technology.

The Summer Theatre Festival and
Workshop provides a unique bridge
from the academic to the professional.
Here theatre students may apply the
skills developed in the classroom
through working and learning from a
professional company. In recent years
the Trinity Square Players and the
Theatre Company of Boston have
been in residence.

The B.A. program is designed for the
student who wishes to prepare himself
for a career as a scholar in theatre,
or who wishes to use theatre as a
standard academic major. A special
program in Theatre Education is
offered under the B.A. in cooperation
with the Department of Education for
students who wish to teach theatre
on the secondary school level.

Black and Gray Called
Black and White

Printing a black and white photograph well is usually more difficult than printing a painting in a wide range of colors. We accept reproduction in color as facsimile; for an artist's black and white photograph we look for precise duplication.

It is especially difficult to achieve acceptable reproduction for an artist such as Aaron Siskind. He pushes the density and diversity of blacks to the limit. A reproduction that distorts the original tones seriously reduces the integrity of the photograph and diminishes its power.

We call these photographs black and white, white being the color of the paper. To sensitive eyes, there is a wide and intricate range of tones.

In order to capture these subtle variations, such work is usually printed with two colors of ink, black and gray, by a process called duotone or slid dot. This double-dot printing helps achieve the depth and tonal nuance of the original. The amount of gray or black ink needed to reproduce an artist's set of photographs may vary from image to image. In some cases, the blacks must be printed several times to accomplish an accurate array of tones.

Double-page Spreads 1990
National Museum of American Art,
Smithsonian Institution

Harlem Document, Photographs 1932–1940:
Aaron Siskind

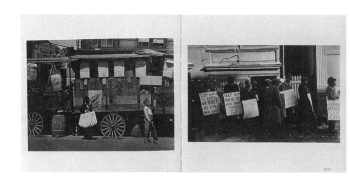

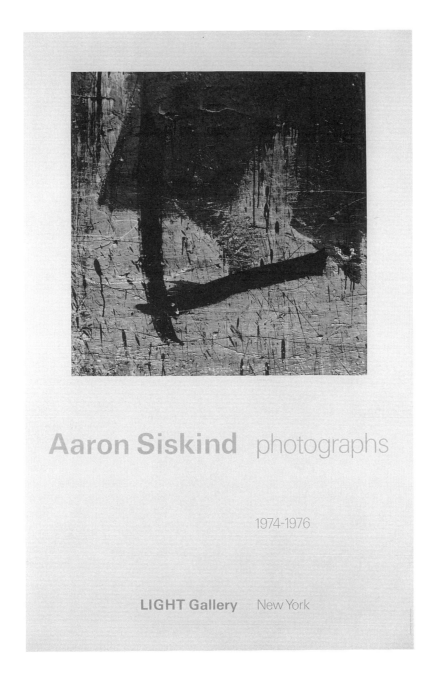

Layering

Brochure Cover 1972
Mt. Holyoke College

By changing the size of dots within the pattern, we get an illusion of space and mystery.

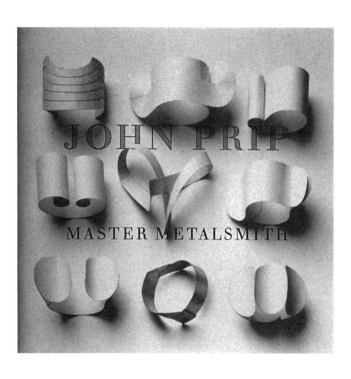

Catalogue Cover 1987
Museum of Art
Rhode Island School of Design

The artist first did paper models before doing each piece in silver for this cover. I used photographs of these models, printed in silver ink. Type placed partly behind the image establishes a dimension that did not exist in the original photograph.

Depending on the amount of reflected light that reaches the viewer's eyes, the silver images emerge and fade as the viewing angle changes.

Double-page Spread 1987
Moliterno Stone Sales

Double-page spread from a brochure for a stone cutter.

The layering of images suggests the application of the cut stone that this company produces.

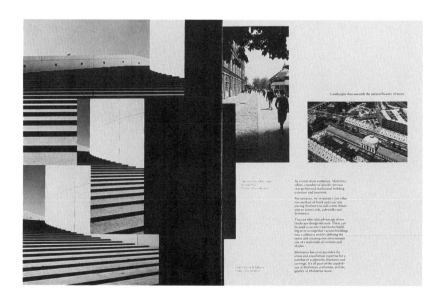

Announcement Poster 1974
Monumenta

This poster announced an exhibition of monumental sculpture along Ocean View Drive in Newport, Rhode Island.

We designed the poster before any piece was selected for the exhibit. The open space, slightly skewed by the overlaying of an image of itself, suggests that something is to be placed within it but exactly what it will be remains uncertain, mysterious, open to imagination.

Well, He Was A Great Talker, You Know.

...Let The Nation Know

Being a porter was educational

So I Selected Boston.

The Essence of Trade Unionism

When I Left The Railroad

Being A Porter Was Educational

because of the traveling. And it was a clean job. You had your nice uniform, white shirt, and black tie. And, well, you felt like an executive. I served famous people, the Rockefeller family, the old man Rockefeller. And I had Jackie Robinson on my train.

Theron Brown, Porter

So I Selected Boston.

Came to Boston, right...to Back Bay Station with my baggage. Got in a cab and asked the guy to take me to the colored section.

Elsa Henderson, Dining Car Waiter

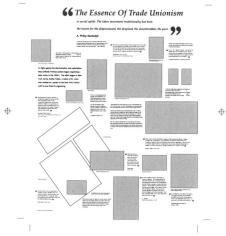

The Essence Of Trade Unionism

is social uplift. The labor movement traditionally has been the haven for the dispossessed, the despised, the downtrodden, the poor.

A. Philip Randolph

...Let The Nation Know

the meaning of our numbers. We are not a pressure group, we are not an organization...we are not a mob. We are the advance guard of a massive moral revolution for jobs and freedom...But this civil rights revolution is not confined to the Negro, nor is it confined to civil rights, for our white allies know that they are not free while we are not...

A. Philip Randolph

Exhibition Panels 1991
A. Philip Randolph Exhibit
Massachusetts Bay Transportation Authority

Six porcelain and enamel commemorative
panels showing the history of A. Philip Randolph
and his efforts to unionize black railroad
workers. The exhibit is on permanent display
at the Back Bay Station in Boston and was part
of Black History Month.

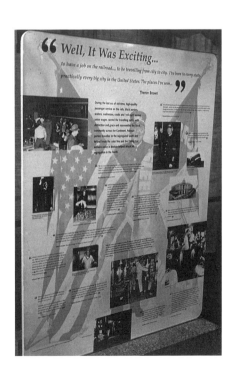

When I was asked to design a poster to be shown in Hiroshima on the anniversary of th dropping of the atomic bomb, I was remind of the newspaper articles and advertisement from World War II and the Vietnam War. In t latter case, students and faculty were desig ing and printing posters and getting them or the streets an hour later. I was influenced by the coarseness of the halftone dots in these quick and grainy productions.

I wanted to recapture the feeling of newspaper-like immediacy—harsh, colloquia and blunt—suggesting time, space, and movement.

I felt that a poster on this grim topic should avoid the sleek "beauty" one sees in ads for expensive cars or perfumes.

During World War II, a familiar diagram showed three concentric circles, the smallest circle in the center indicating ground zero, where the most damage had been done. If one bomb is dropped, it will bring retaliation producing Earth Zero—no earth.

A simple concept, but it took nineteen layers of acetate sheets to prepare the finished art. The word "Peace" is printed in Japanese calligraphy.

ROGER WILLIAMS COLLEGE
ARCHITECTURE BUILDING

Brochure Cover 1988
Roger Williams College

We try here to show some of the architectural detail of the building, which is essentially without ornament.

EARTH
ZERO

平
和

Design by Malcolm Grear. Screen Printing by Bizzarro

Announcement 1983
Union College

Since the pieces on exhibit covered such a broad range, rather than using an actual example of our work, we used an image that is meant to convey a sense of order, clarity, and care.

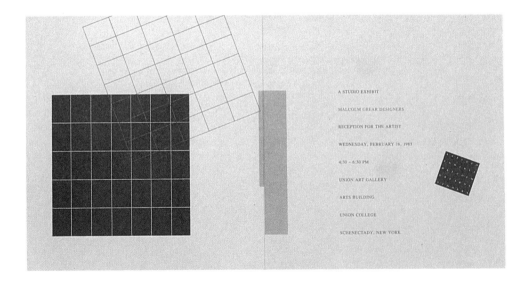

One of a Kind

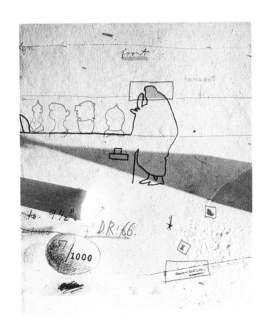

Catalogue Covers 1966
Museum of Art
Rhode Island School of Design

A collaborative effort with Diter Rot. We produced one thousand catalogues for a "Still Life Exhibition." Each cover was unique.

We, including Diter Rot, stamped various images, drawn by Diter Rot, on a reproduction of another drawing by Diter Rot and then added other personal touches—painting, drawing, writing. Diter then signed each cover.

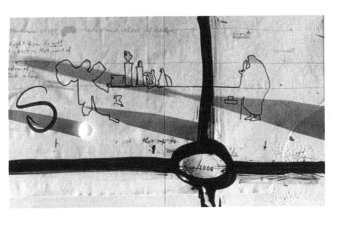

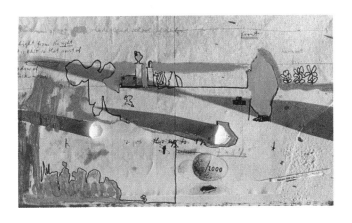

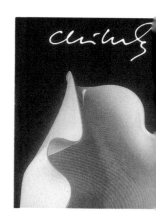

Poster 1977
Dale Chihuly

We used the signature not just because it
is Dale's but because its free-flowing form
relates so nicely to the art itself.

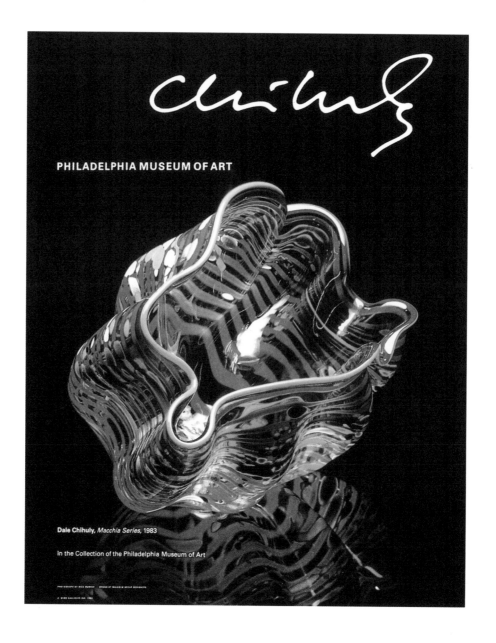

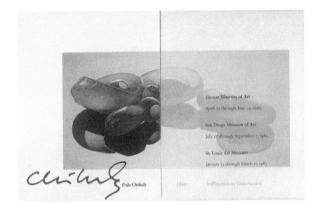

Book 1982
Dale Chihuly

Cover and five double-page spreads.

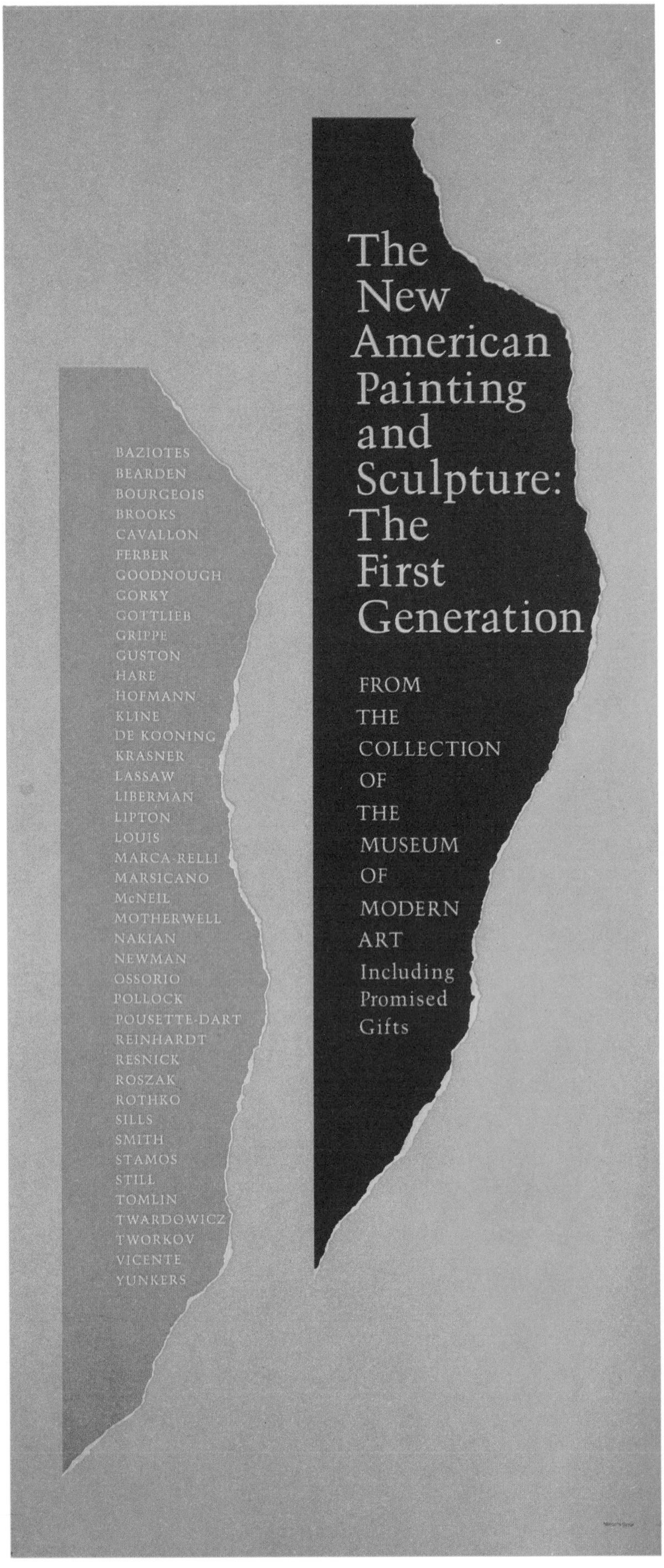

Poster 1969
The Museum of Modern Art, New York

We used a simple device in this poster to evoke the work of artists who had been labeled hard edge or soft edge painters and sculptors.

An interesting torn edge may seem simple to achieve; we found it strangely difficult. A frustratingly large number of tears were made before we got what we thought would work.

The
New
American
Painting
and
Sculpture:
The
First
Generation

FROM
THE
COLLECTION
OF
THE
MUSEUM
OF
MODERN
ART
Including
Promised
Gifts

BAZIOTES
BEARDEN
BOURGEOIS
BROOKS
CAVALLON
FERBER
GOODNOUGH
GORKY
GOTTLIEB
GRIPPE
GUSTON
HARE
HOFMANN
KLINE
DE KOONING
KRASNER
LASSAW
LIBERMAN
LIPTON
LOUIS
MARCA-RELLI
MARSICANO
McNEIL
MOTHERWELL
NAKIAN
NEWMAN
OSSORIO
POLLOCK
POUSETTE-DART
REINHARDT
RESNICK
ROSZAK
ROTHKO
SILLS
SMITH
STAMOS
STILL
TOMLIN
TWARDOWICZ
TWORKOV
VICENTE
YUNKERS

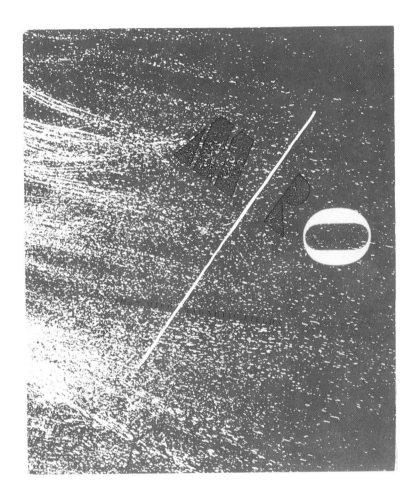

Catalogue Cover 1972
The Solomon R. Guggenheim Museum

Here we come upon one of those famous
thin lines.

I attempted to show on the cover some of the
things Joan Miro had meant to me for so
many years, the ways he had handled space,
movement, and dimension.

This is dangerous work for a designer; it is
disturbingly easy to *imitate* rather than represent so powerful an artist.

Sequencing, Relating, and Pacing

A book or catalogue should be designed from inside to outside, beginning with its content. If the book presents an artist's work, the nature of this work will determine graphic presentation of preface, acknowledgments, essays, cover, and all other elements.

We first design the main body of the book, then we do the front and back matter, the endpapers and, finally, the cover, which must somehow convey a sense of the entire work.

The visual "poetry" of a book is formed by the pacing or flow of images and type. If a book has weak or muddled visual structure, its information loses force. A layout can be so busy,

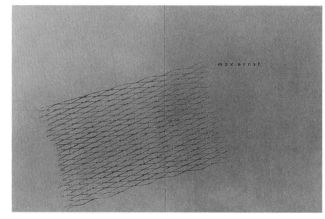

Book walk.

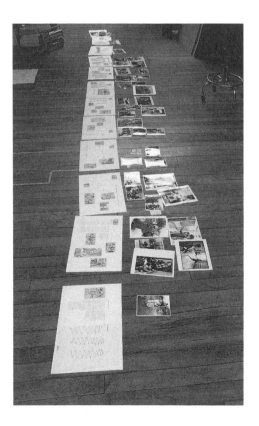

Catalogue 1975
The Solomon R. Guggenheim Museum

The placement of type and image in the catalogue for Max Ernst shows variation from one spread to the next even though a grid structure is used to unify the elements.

so self important, that the reader has trouble tracking content. Or the structure can be so tight that words and images take on an unwelcoming coldness and density not native to the content.

If the designer's "system" is rigidly dictatorial, then the pattern of type, image, and space will show no diversity from page to page. The end result will be boredom, the ascendance of system over substance. A system of specifications should be flexible enough to allow changes when content demands; systems should accommodate subsystems; there should be enough relaxation to engender surprise and delight.

These general notions mainly apply to picture books, books of words can also benefit from varied pattern within the discipline of a consistent format.

For art books pacing is critical. If a light, soft drawing is placed next to a bold one, each can drain significance from the other. If two images with similar color and form are on facing pages, the viewer may see them almost as one, and neither will receive the attention needed to catch its essence. There is always some loss of power when an image is bunched together with its fellows, in a book or an exhibit, which is partly why we often are struck more deeply by a picture seen in a home rather than in a gallery or book.

The designer should begin by understanding as much as possible about the art and artist and what is being written about both. This application of the principle of inside/outside is, in my view, of fundamental value for any designer, any design.

When the designer understands the work and builds upon this understanding, effective pacing, with intriguing surprises, will keep the reader involved. Visual energy must be sustained from start to finish. Don't blow all strength in the beginning or lump it in the middle or save it for the end.

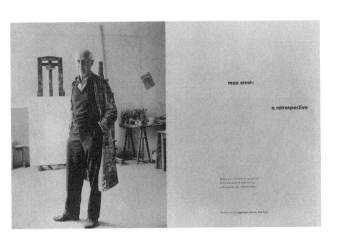

One good way to plan pacing is to place the illustrations in a row, one next to the other. Then move images around, changing relationships until you feel comfortable with them. (Sometimes images must be arranged in chronological order or must follow some other constraint.) Then place the images in a progression of double-page spreads, leaving blank spaces when no image seems appropriate.

Next, design a system based on this array.

A book is best designed as a series of double-page spreads. If you lay these spreads next to each other on the floor, you can then "walk" the spreads, going up and down the row, moving the images, changing scale relationships, and so on.

We usually tape these double-page spreads together to form an accordion fold, allowing us to look at several spreads at once or to turn the pages like those in an ordinary book.

Sometimes I devise a numerical code to check the pattern. Thus, number 1 might stand for a single image that spans a double-page spread; 2 for a single image next to a blank page; 3 for a single image next to a page of solid color; 4 for an image on each page of a spread; 5 for more than two images on a spread. The total sequence then reveals the pacing at a glance; for example 5, 3, 2, 2, 1, 4, 4, 1, 5, 2, 3, 4. If this order, when read aloud, seems to have a faulty rhythm, I look back at the layout to see if changes need to be made. This is strictly a personal method, in some ways nonsensical, but I find it helpful. It prompts me to consider the whole sequence, and it often signals the need for adjustment.

When determining sequence for the two books shown, consisting mainly of photographs, several things were considered simultaneously: visual connections, patterns, repetition.

Book 1980
Aperture

These pages, from a book of Brett Weston's photographs, are shown in sequence.

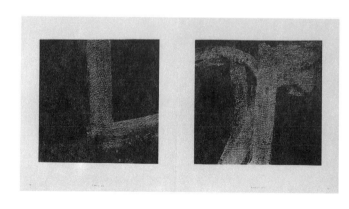

Book 1976
Aaron Siskind

These pages, from a book of Aaron Siskind's photographs, show pacing of the images.

All the photographs are beautiful. Not all can be included. How does one select? It is a troubling responsibility. You can become deeply involved in the inner forms and spend hours in front of just one print.

One tries for a balance of form and meaning. One also tries for an easy flow of space, revealing the grace of each image page by page.

No general reader is likely to be aware of these details, which is just as well. One wants the reader to experience the work itself, not the design. A good movie or novel sweeps you into the story. You may be fleetingly conscious of artistic strategy from time to time, but the mechanics of the work are for the most part obscured by the power of the art itself. So it is with the design of a book and the design of much else that we use day by day.

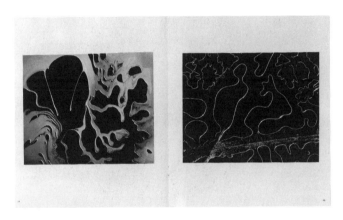

College Textbook 1989
Worth Publishers

Readers are affected by design, even if they don't know it. This is particularly true of college textbooks. All other things being equal (the quality of the writing, for example) a student will find a well designed text easier to follow than one that is visually dull, densely packed with type and lackluster illustrations.

Professors, too, are influenced by a textbook's appearance. It is they who choose which book their students must buy. When a publisher sends a professor a free copy for examination in hopes that the professor will adopt the text, that publisher stands a better chance against competitors if the book is nicely put together. Scholarly virtues count for a lot, of course, but there is no question that good design is good marketing and good teaching.

How does the book look (and feel, since texture matters) inside and outside? Is it inviting? Is the information arranged clearly? Is the type easy to read? Are the illustrations well displayed and placed close to the relevant text? Is color used to clarify rather than adorn?

The college textbooks we have designed during the last twenty-four years, essentially all of them for Worth Publishers, have been notably successful teaching tools because authors, editors, illustrators, and designers have collaborated in a mood of inventive concern for the student reader's needs.

When the editors at Worth, a new start-up publisher, called to talk about our designing their first book, they were laboring under the radical view that textbooks should look like art books. Although I had bent their ears with my criticism of current textbook design, I had to assert my conviction that textbooks should not look like art books anymore than art books should look like textbooks.

But we understood each other. They wanted to publish textbooks of high quality and they had the wit to realize that this effort must include design.

Back then, in the mid-sixties, most science textbooks, while containing fascinating information about the way the world works, looked dreary and boring. Books were turned out in standard formats. All subjects seemed to be treated the same way, whether biology or auto mechanics. Illustrations were routine. Color, if used at all, was there

for visual flash. Some of these flaws persist, but the industry has improved. There is a growing sense of the value, pedagogical and commercial, of good design.

A first step in textbook design, as with all book design, is to discover what the author and publisher want to achieve. You have to get into the manuscript, read chunks of it, whether physics or music, and try to catch the essence of the subject, the power and beauty it holds for the author, which the book must impart to the student.

If the market is competitive, why another book? What does the author have to say that others have not already said? What are the budgetary constraints?

After several discussions with author and editor, you begin to understand their purposes and their strengths.

Once you understand the book as a whole and know for whom it is intended, the design begins to take shape. By this time you will have a structure that accommodates all components: the number of sections, chapters, different levels of information within chapters, chapter openers, chapter outlines, lists, extracts, art and captions, tables, end-of-chapter questions and summaries, bibliography, glossary, appendices, and so on.

Then you choose a typeface that suits the subject. Deal first with the most complex situations. One section may consist of running text with lengthy paragraphs and very few heads; another may have short paragraphs with many heads, charts, diagrams, photographs, drawings, essays, and other elements. Each element must be clearly distinguished but be in visual harmony with all others.

We prepare a layout of the book, with as many pages as it takes to show the flow, the visual progression. If you turn three or four pages, you may become aware of part of the structure; it takes many more turns to sense the whole layout.

Once the initial design has been evaluated and approved, we write comprehensive specifications and roughly calculate the total number of pages. Then we prepare a "dummy" book to hold and feel and turn the pages. Size and weight are major concerns. If the book is too thick, it might intimidate.

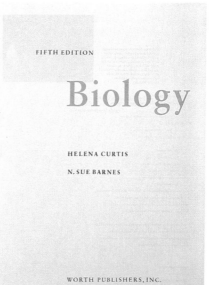

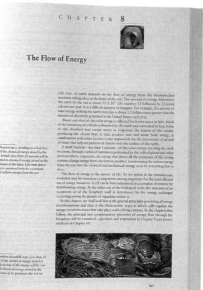

The design is adjusted as manuscript development proceeds. We try to assure that illustrations are located on the same page as the related text or on the facing page. It is no easy task to design a system that accommodates this constraint in a natural way, particularly if there are many illustrations accompanying a short bit of text.

In the best of circumstances, the designer will establish the style for illustrations, making sure that form, color, and line weight are compatible with the design, and will work with author and publisher to select the best artist and photographer for the project.

The designer must care about production costs. The more colors you print, usually two to five, the more expensive the book will be. Adding half an inch to the height can have a major effect on production costs and selling price.

While cost control is very important, content and function are the main determinants of book design. If, for example, an unusual height, within reason, or the addition of colors, will make the book more useful, the designer should plead the case.

The color palette, for use in solid, line, type, and background, must be designed so that each color is pleasing and ef-

fective in a wide range of percentage amounts and in combination with other colors. Five percent of a certain red could end up looking like bubble gum pink. Two colors when printed together could end up looking like mud.

When I was in grade school, the first assignment that the teacher gave us after passing out new books was to take them home and have our parents help us cover them, usually with a cut-up brown paper bag, neatly taped or glued around the book—no glue on the books, of course. This was my first experience with book jackets.

College Textbook 1970
Worth Publishers

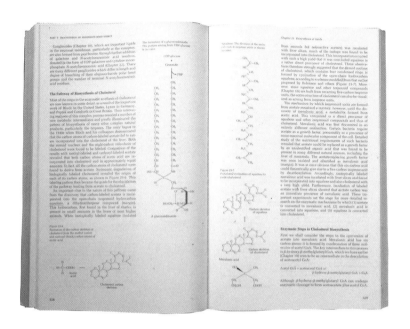

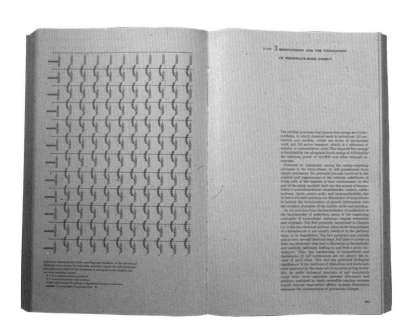

As the year wore on, those jackets became more and more interesting, alive with all sorts of drawings, symbols, and secret messages.

Designing covers for textbooks is problematic: Too many people have too much to say about their appearance. Authors; publishers; editors; production, marketing and sales people. It is like selling detergent, if blue and yellow is a grabber, make it blue and yellow.

The designer must fight to have the cover connect soundly to the inside of the book.

The shape of the biochemistry textbook, a tall, narrow format, allowing molecular forms to fit in the margins, helped the publisher obtain adoptions. The book immediately became a best seller in its field. The quality of the author's manuscript, of course had a lot to do with this success; but the design played a significant role in launching the book and in its didactic value as a tool for students taking a first course in biochemistry.

Even though the designer must seek economy, it cannot always be the determining factor. This format was not the most economical size for printing. But it improved the exposition and boosted sales.

Today typography is computerized. The first book we designed was set in metal type. The typographic format was based on two measures: The widest, with flush left and right margins, was used for the body text; this same measure and a narrower one, in italics, flush left and ragged right, was used for captions.

The book was mainly typeset in wide measure, with the option of sliding the wide captions to the left. The narrow captions were used for side illustrations. The illustrations, drawn by Shirley Batey, have line weights and proportions that we had specified.

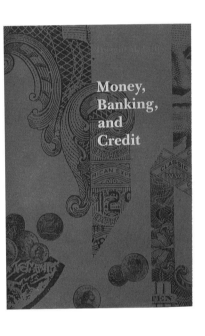

College Textbook 1989
Worth Publishers

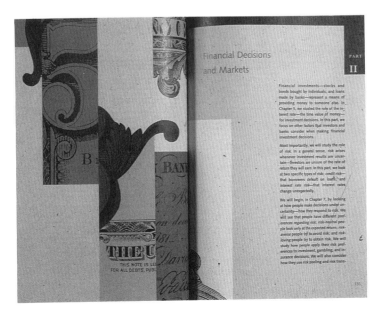

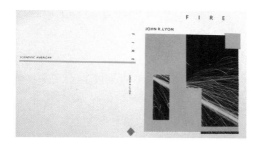

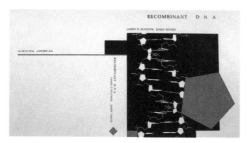

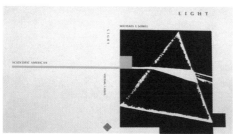

A Series 1982
Scientific American Library

This series is intended for readers of Scientific American magazine. Each topic is written by an expert; many are Nobel laureates. Full-color paintings and photographs help make the science clear.

Six volumes are published each year.

We first designed the series format.

Included on this page are some of the ideas we rejected because, while attractive, they seemed too "temporary."

After we got a form that we liked, we designed a grid to suit a variety of subject matter. The series covers topics across all sciences.

We designed the first nineteen books in the series. On subsequent books, the publisher followed our design.

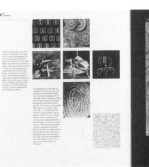

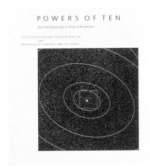

Powers of Ten was the first book in the series. There is a definite structure followed throughout, but its use is varied from page to page.

Horizontal and Vertical

Brochure 1980
Moran Industries

A brochure that explains the capabilities of a Louisiana printing firm.

We chose jazz as a theme because of the firm's location. Also, some of the same words used in the printing trade are used in jazz — progression, color, tone, variation, and so on.

Normally a catalogue, brochure, or book has either a horizontal or vertical progression, from right to left or top to bottom. In this example, the design operates horizontally and vertically. The art in the brochure was also used on a poster, by placing one double-page spread over the other.

The poster became a follow-up mailing. We were told that those who received these pieces didn't throw them away. They suggested the rhythms of jazz while giving information about Moran Printing.

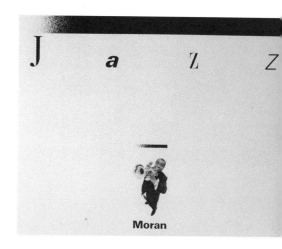

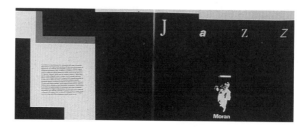

Capabilities Brochure 1990
Graham Gund Architects

This brochure, which serves as the company's profile, highlights their accomplishments. The format reflects their spirited architecture. The color, texture, and patterns of their work are woven into the design. The informal grid allows flexibility in the layout of each page, a flexibility that resonates with the personality and approach of Graham Gund Architects, an inventive design firm.

The brochure is read at three levels: photography, text, and quotations by clients, critics, and the general public. We focus on the photographs and renderings. Decorative accents are understated; pastel tones form the background for details from some of their projects.

The folder and note card are integral parts of the initial package. The folder, which holds magazine and newspaper reprints, is restrained in color and design so that it does not compete with the brochure. The folder is also a separate mailing piece.

The purpose of the note card is twofold: To invite the reader to contact the firm and to announce the firm's twentieth anniversary.

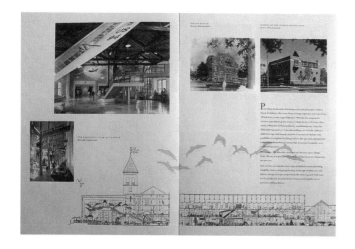

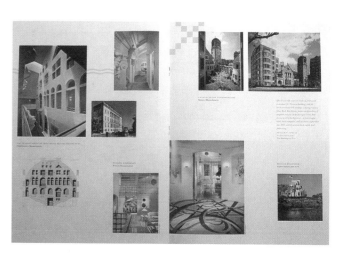

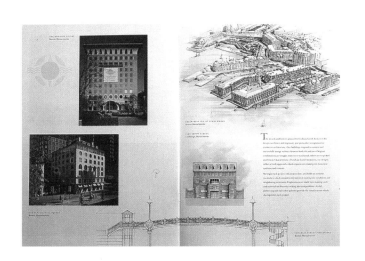

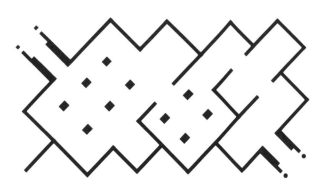

Space Plan

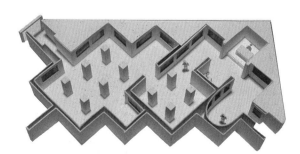

Space Model

Exhibition Design

A grid plan is useful for planning space and scale relationships.

Modular units make it easy to add or remove sections.

Walk-through Exhibit 1986
Mayo Clinic, Jacksonville

An exhibit of historical achievements, recent developments, and plans for the future.

Donor Recognition Room 1990
Mayo Clinic, Rochester

The Donor Recognition Room at the Mayo Foundation displays, in alphabetic order, the names of those who have contributed to the foundation. Our design demonstrates the foundation's respect for these benefactors and its continuing gratitude for their support.

We used slate, a durable substance, as one device to express enduring appreciation. Each donor's name is etched into a slat made of slate. The slats slide into frames; new names can be inserted while retaining the alphabetic scheme.

The result is a permanent array of names that allows new names to be added. Each category of donor has its own color of slate—red, green, and black—which produces an intriguing random pattern.

Storyboard Model

Exhibit 1983
Museum of the USS Constitution

An exhibit on the life of Isaac Hull, Captain
of the USS Constitution (Old Ironsides).
Considerable historic material — artifacts,
paintings, and documents — required a system
of display that affords opportunity for easy
change. Display modules, copy, and lighting
allow flexibility.

Beyond Structure

Street Marker 1987
Tufts University School of Medicine

A street marker designed to signal the location of the university's first medical school.

The pattern for the existing brick plaza provided a natural solution to the problem.

We chose a theme that evokes the texture of the original building.

To form the marker, bricks were removed and cast in bronze. A single black marble brick with hand drawn, inlaid numbers shows the date of the original building. The combination of metal and stone conveys durability.

Workers prepare the site for installation.

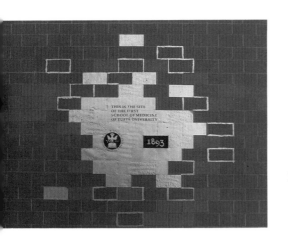

When presenting the concept, we used colored paper, gold foils, crayon, and paint.

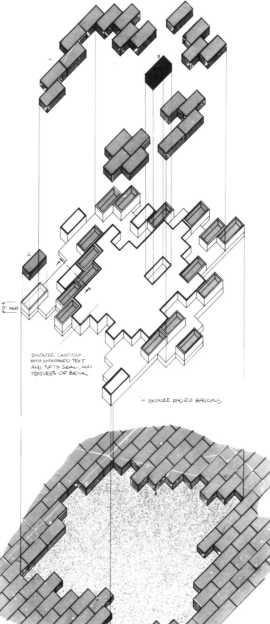

Workers prepare the marker for installatio

A drawing illustrates the fit of bronze and brick.

A detail of the marker.

A view showing the marker's integration with the plaza.

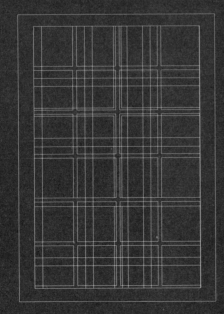

Doing This Book

Ideas for this book were churning in my head for a long time before I began putting them on paper.

Once I had chosen illustrations and written a rough draft, I did sketches of a design. I built a structure based on these sketches and made pages of text and images, using photocopies of the actual materials.

After I had done all of this, the design seemed too loose and unstructured.

I prepared a second design, but this one did not accommodate the words and images in a natural manner; it was strained and stiff. I prepared several other designs before I settled on the one you now see. The trim size of the book and its general format grew out of the content, from inside to outside. I did not choose an arbitrary size to fit printing presses or standard sheets of paper.

Once I felt comfortable with the overall pattern of type and illustrations, I prepared small sketches of every page. I could then see the whole series of pages all at once. I am a relic from the past who still sketches layouts by hand instead of manipulating electronic visions on a computer screen.

After the grid sheets were printed, my daughter Leah, following my sketches, layed out every page. She designed several pages on her own, using the structure as a guide. We revised many times.

Leah and I had several "book walks," spreading pages along the floor of the hallway to check sequence, flow, progression, juxtaposition.

As for the writing, it was tough. I rewrote every sentence several times. Still you will find, as I do, the sounds and rhythms of a Kentucky country boy whose natural language is shape, space and color. The English language, which I dearly love, is not my bread and butter.

Studies for a symbol to represent the
Providence Journal Company.

A Way of Working

Some class assignments have taken me years to develop, and development continues. Anyone who has taught design knows that the same assignment given by two teachers will not be the same educational experience for the students. This principle holds when a teacher gives the same assignment to different students. The cliche is correct: "You can't step in the same river twice."

If a design assignment is well conceived, you get as many different solutions as you have students, unless it is a strictly mechanical exercise. Former students, now teachers, assign some of the exercises I assigned to them. And, of course, some of my assignments grow from ideas my mentors passed to me. Thus are traditions sustained from generation to generation, continuity within the flow.

The exercises in this book are springboards, jumping-off points; the experience a student gains by doing them has applicability across a wide range of problems.

The professional projects at the end of the book are my attempt to demonstrate approaches to solving problems in design. Each project undertaken by our studio leaves a residue of insight, however amorphous, that is useful in subsequent work. We do learn from experience.

Most solutions are shaped by the boundaries of a problem. Constraints become the mothers of invention. So much in nature is formed by necessity, but mindlessly.

Designs are likewise subject to imperatives—form and function interacting.

When I began this book, I presumed to become my own client, a dangerous liaison if ever there was one. As might be expected, the designer became exasperated with the client, who was just as often fed up with the designer. With frequent episodes of vanity and stubbornness, we struggled to the finish.

Nothing, of course, is timeless. Design, along with everything else, occurs in history and reflects the days of its origin. I am not at ease with this natural law and always try to transcend fashion. My rational self recognizes the futility of this conceit, but I remain emotionally bound to the ancient quest for durable achievement. I try for permanence, if not for the objects I design, at least for the forms and principles I apply. Quality, a deeply subjective construct, remains my muse. There is no logic here, but I find solace in the ambition.

Learning to Listen

Shortly after my graduation from design school, the president of a printing firm called to ask if I would design an identity program for his firm. He wanted a symbol that would go on stationery and related materials and on a sign for his building.

I tried to be cool as I assured him that he had called the right person.

The evening before our appointment, I slicked up the portfolio and got ready to show my potential client God's gift to the world of design.

When I arrived, a secretary took me to the president's office and seated me in a chair centered in front of his desk, my unblemished portfolio placed carefully beside me on the floor.

He walked in without saying hello, glanced at my portfolio, and said, "I don't need to see your work, I know what I want, a picture of Benjamin Franklin and his printing press."

I picked up my portfolio and made for the door, saying, "You design it, I'll bill you for it."

I was fool enough to bill him; he was smart enough not to pay.

The delights of arrogance are fleeting. I soon regained some vestige of sense and saw that I was the loser. I had wanted to design an image for a real company. What could have been better than doing one for a printer?

Since that day I have held the congenial notion that almost no idea a client proposes is entirely cornball; it's what you do with it.

I now listen to any idea a client proposes. If I do my job well, I can learn from the client and the client can learn from me.

Other Lessons Learned

Several years ago, while we were designing a trademark and identity program for a large corporation, the corporate communications director happened to be visiting Providence and dropped by the studio.

It was during a euphoric stage when we were really smokin'; many studies, part of our research for the project, were floating around the studio. I let my excitement get the best of me and showed him some of the studies. He was impressed; he had no idea that anyone would go to such lengths to develop a visual identity for his or any corporation.

Early the following week he called to say how impressed he was and asked if I would gather some of the studies, hop on a plane, come to corporate headquarters, and show this impressive stuff to the chairman of the board.

I told him that we were just beginning and had not arrived at any decision. He said he understood and just wanted to show the chairman that we were doing substantial work, not just whipping something out.

We mounted several studies on boards and I flew to meet the boss.

I arrived at headquarters and rehearsed my presentation with the communications director. As I was showing him the boards, he pointed to one and said, "That's wonderful, that's it!"

I reminded him that we had not finished the study and that no choice should be made until we had done so. He agreed.

We walked upstairs to the president's office and placed the presentation boards around the room so that the chairman could see some of what goes into making an identity program.

While we were doing this, the president pointed to the one that the communications director had liked and said, "That's it, that will look great on the corporate jet."

I pointed out, as politely as possible, that "We are not designing an identity program for the corporate plane; it's for the corporation, and these examples are only a few from the total study."

The chairman of the board came into the room, walked straight to the same symbol and said, "That's it!" Again I went through my spiel.

I was then given a good-humored lecture about my lack of business acumen. They would pay me without my having to do more work on this phase of the project. The chairman considered this a good deal for me.

I returned to their headquarters the following week and spent most of the day talking them out of the image that all three had singled out. And I succeeded.

Alas, by the end of our studio's research, I wanted to settle on the very one the executives had liked in the first place; but it was too late—I had done too good a job convincing them that it wasn't right!

The lesson: You will not know which design is best until you have completed a thorough study, so don't decide for *or against* any version while you are still in the midst of it. A corollary: Clients sometimes know best.

We have often gone through numerous studies, hundreds of drawings, only to come back to our first idea. We seldom fix on that idea in unaltered form, but we frequently use it as a point of departure in a new line of development that leads to a satisfactory resolution.

A view into the studio at home.

Joy

One of my brightest joys, directly flowing from my work in design, is the forever stimulating interaction with clients and collaborators. How did a boy from rural Kentucky come to work on level ground with scholars of all sorts—mathematicians, physicists, chemists, biologists, economists, nobel laureates—men and women of mental grace well beyond my own, corporate leaders, sculptors, painters, curators of great collections, museum directors, publishers, architects, engineers, master craftsmen, women and men of great intellectual and social power? This has been, still is, deeply satisfying communion with a set of vital people, all of whom know much more about what they do than I could hope to know. I join them in social and professional discourse because I presume to meet them on equal footing. I do design. They do commerce, management, art, publishing, architecture, science, whatever. They need me; I need them.

I am a lucky man. Not by design, but through design, I have gained a life of friendships, respectful affections, delightful collaborations—all born of my work, which in itself, in its daily texture and visual diversity, brings pleasure to my soul. I have found my way. There is nothing I would rather do than graphic design. This is not to say that I have found safe harbor. I'm still on the open sea. It's just that I love it out here.

There are, of course, many other joys (my prairie flower, my children, their children; and jokes. I love jokes—hearing them and telling them). Another source of good feeling is the art in my rooms at home: Chihuly's cylinders and shells of glass, Natkin's layered skins of color, Townley's bold wood forms, Ives' letterforms, Aki's crayoned leaves, Callahan's trees and grasses, Siskind's rocks, all sorts of images, forms, structures, patterns, and substances. What music meant to Mozart these objects mean to me.

Coda

I began this book with an assignment on "The Form of a Maple Leaf," in which I ask students to draw a realistic version of this familiar botanical object. Understandably, they render sketchy approximations, often charming but usually wide of the mark. They do not yet know that leaf from the inside out; they do not yet see how the outer form is shaped by inner form and the interrelated functions of its parts. I end my account of this exercise with a general principle: "there is no substitute for knowledge about the object or process one is attempting to convey through graphic design."

Over the past three decades I have spent thousands of hours with students. During that time I have tried to follow my own advice, to study *them*, as it were, from the inside out. I do not know them, of course, the way one can know a leaf, a hugely ornate system that traps sunlight to build the living plant. How much more bewilderingly complex is a human being, a student in quest of competence, searching for experience, subduing fears, yearning to create? I don't pretend to know how learning occurs, how the creative process unfolds. But one thing seems clear. The more I work with students, witness their originality, the more I recognize that my didactic labor is not the most important process going on in the classroom. At best, I open a few doors, pick a few locks. The students carry within them so much force and vision, so many ideas. I just help them, now and then, to release these imaginings.

There is a persistent paradigm of education, the "tabula rasa" scheme, which regards students as empty slates that instructors fill with information. I find more realistic the notion that each of us comes into the world with a certain nature, a mix of aptitudes and talents that, while similar to those of all humankind, is particular to ourselves. In this model, education, although imparting specific information—the physiology of a leaf, for example—is primarily a procedure whereby the teacher *respectfully* draws from students that which is uniquely within their own minds, hearts, and spirits. This I have found to be a gradual process, a kind of flowering. I sometimes think that my work in the classroom is more like gardening than teaching.

I read recently a study showing that people from diverse places around the world, when shown pictures of a wide variety of landscapes—mountains, forest, meadows, seaside, and so on—and asked to select their favorite, overwhelmingly choose pictures that echo the savannas of our origin, open grassland with a few scattered trees and some water. The argument goes that this common affinity for a particular pattern of natural scenery is built into the human mind. I am not, I think no one is, suggesting that there is a gene for landscape preference, but I like the romantic idea that our species evolved over millions of years and our minds carry inherent information and tendencies.

These speculations may seem irrelevant in a book about design, but the main point, that we come into the world with inherent ways, does bear on my work or, at least, my view of that work. For I am persuaded that design, like music, language, mathematics, art, science (curiosity), and the rest, is part of the structure of the mind. Doing design, responding to design—to shapes, textures, and colors in space—has played and continues to play a part in the survival of our kind. Design, done by nature with blind but dazzling elegance (the leaf, again) and by us with human purpose, is no mere cultural confection; it is in us.

This "reality" affects my professional practice. I run a design studio; my name is on the door; I presume to manage the enterprise. It is humbling to contemplate the true character of this role as "manager", a term that ranks with "teacher" in the lexicon of common terms commonly misconstrued. Aside from directing mundane financial and logistical operations, my managing, like my teaching, mostly consists of encouraging others, in this case my colleagues, to trust their skills and intuitions, to explore and express the ideas that spring to mind, to join their peers in collaborative effort, to try to see the world from the clients perspective and take to heart the purposes our designs are meant to serve. There is harmony, usually, within our collaboration because we have come to know each other well enough to see what each does best, and worst, and because we improve these observations over time and apply them to our shared effort as designers. We work from the inside out.

Index

A

Accordion fold, 66, 72–73
Anniversary poster:
    Earth Zero, 258–59
    Simpson, Francis and Virgil, 247
Announcement:
    Monumenta poster, 255
    Providence Art Club, 230
    Union College, 260
Art Academy of Cincinnati, 15
Audubon Society of Rhode Island,
    symbols/signs, 164–67

B

Balance, 26, 242–47
Banco de Edwards, symbol, 200
Batey, Shirley, 273
Bay State Abrasives, symbol, 195
Big Canoe, directional sign, 239
Boghosian, Varujan, 182
Book design, 266–73
    layout, 270
    and manuscript development, 272
    museum catalogue, 266–67
    pacing, 267–68
    photography books, 268–69
    readers and, 270
    sequencing, 266–67, 268
    steps in, 270–73
Boston City Hospital, signs, 202–3
Brier Manufacturing, symbol, 192
Brown Daltas & Associates, theme
    and variations, 266–27
Brown University:
    poster, 231
    University press, symbol, 194

C

Cannon Design, symbol, 208
Catalogue cover and poster, Museum
    of Art, Rhode Island School of
    Design, 248–49
Catalogue covers, Museum of Art,
    Rhode Island School of Design,
    254, 261
Chairforms, 40–43
Chihuly, Dale:
    book, 263
    double-page spread, 263
    exhibition poster, 246, 262
Color Concentrate Corporation,
    symbol, 184
Community Preparatory School,
    symbol/promotional materials,
    210
Computer, and electronic
    composition, 143
Constantly moving symbols, 209
Containers/contents, 134–35
Counterform/form, 184–89
    posters, 186–89
    symbols, 184–85
Cover designs, college textbooks, 273

D

Daltas, Spero, 226–27
Dartmouth College, poster, 220–21, 232
Department of Architecture, Rhode
    Island School of Design, poster,
    188–89
Department of Health and Human
    Services, symbol, 184
Design commissions, 183–285
    balance, 242–47
    beyond structure, 284–85
    black and white, 248–51
    black and gray called black and
    white, 252–53
    constantly moving symbols, 209
    counterform/form, 184–89
    dual visual meaning, 200–203
    exhibition design, 281, 282–83
    expanded meaning, 206–8

function following form, 226–27
graphics standards manual, 216–17
grid, disguising, 278–80
horizontal and vertical, 276–77
humor in design, 210–11
interpretation, 198–99
layering, 254–60
light and shadow, 232–33
light and tension, 197
line, weight, and dimension, 190–93
non-repetitive identity, 218–19
one of a kind, 260
Presbyterian Church (USA), seal and symbol, 212–15
proposal, submitting, 183
scale relationship, 230–31
sequencing, relating, and pacing, 266–73
signs, 233–41
signs without words, 222–25
sun in symbols, 204–5
3/D structure, 282–83
time, space, and position, 228–29
visual switch, 194–96
visual sympathy, 262–65
welcome, 220–21
Designer, *See* Graphic designer
Double-page spread, 70–71, 78, 113, 276–77
Chihuly, Dale, book, 263
Moliterno Stone Sales, 254
National Museum of American Art, Smithsonian Institution, 252
University of Rhode Island, 250–51
Dual visual meaning, 200–203
signs, 202–3
symbols, 200
typographic image, 201

E

Earth Zero, anniversary poster, 258–59
Electronic composition, and computer, 143
Essence of an object, 128–33
Even-step magnifications, 66–67
Exhibition design, 281, 282–83
panels, 256–57
posters, 242–44, 246, 262
walk-through exhibit, 281
Expanded meaning, 206–8

F

Ferrington, Danny, symbol, 206
Field in motion, letterform study, 44–45
Fireworks (Jennings), 148–49
Foremost Lithograph, interior signs, 236–37
Form and structure, 66–87
forms progression, 66–77
juxtaposing images, 80–81
structural framework, 78–79
visual connections/relationships, 82–85
Forms progression, 66–77
accordion fold, 66, 72–73
double-page spread, 70–71, 78
From the Ashes (1960), 16
Furrow, The (1951), 14

G

Graham Gund Architects, capabilities brochure, 278–80
Graphic design, 11–13
as a business, 181
commercial art vs., 11
history of, 11
problem solving in, 289
role of, 13
Graphic designer:
communication of, 12
as problem solver, 13

qualifications/skills of, 179
and typography, 141
Graphic standards manual, 171, 216–17
Grear, Leah, 12, 287
Grear, Malcolm:
From the Ashes (1960), 16
Furrow, The (1951), 14
training, 15
Void (1957), 16
Grid:
and arrangement of composition parts, 78–79
disguising, 278–80
Guggenheim Museum *See* Solomon R. Guggenheim Museum

H

Handtool, function of, 96–64
Harlem Document (Siskind), 156–61
Horizontal and vertical, 276–77
Howell Design Associates, symbol, 190
Hugh Stubbins/Rex Allen partnership, signs, 202–3
Humor in design, 210–11

I

Images, juxtaposing, 80–81
I.M. Pei & Partners, 233
International Institute of Rhode Island, symbols/signs, 169
Interpretation, 198–99
Invisible Cities (Calvino), 152–53
Ives, Norman, 20

J

Jennings, Elizabeth, 148–49
Juxtaposing images, 80–81

K

Koren, Ed, 224–25

L

Layering, 254–60

Layout, book design, 270

Letterforms:

formal qualities of a letter, 46–47

form and structure, 48–65

form of a letter, 24–25

free forms, 26–27

combining structured forms
with, 28–31

letterforms on 3/D surfaces, 32–43

combined chairforms and
letterforms, 43

field in motion, 44–45

form of a chair, 40–41

2/D and 3/D combinations, 34–39

2/D chairform to a 3/D object, 42

letters as forms, 20–24

studies, 20–65

and typography, 140–77

Letters:

formal qualities of, 46–47

as signals, 27

transformation of, 106–9

Light and shadow, 232–33

Light and tension, 197

Light Gallery, poster, 253

Line, weight, and dimension, 190–93

M

Malcolm Grear Designers, 9, 12,
180, 181

Manomet Observatory, symbol, 185

Maple leaf exercise, 18–19, 66

Massachusetts Bay Transportation
Authority (A. Philip Randolph
Exhibit), exhibition panels,
256–57

Mayo Clinic:

donor recognition room, 281

walk-through exhibit, 281

McIlvane, Ed, 215

Merrimack Valley Textile Museum,
symbol, 206

Metropolitan Opera, symbol, 209

Michals, Duane, 163

Mohawk Paper Mills, brochure, 248

Moliterno Stone Sales, double-page
spread, 254

Monumenta, announcement poster, 255

Moran Industries, brochure, 276–77

Morris Museum of Arts and Sciences,
symbol, 211

Mount Holyoke College:

brochure cover, 254

symbol, 184

Museum of Art, Rhode Island School
of Design:

catalogue cover and poster, 248–49

catalogue covers, 254, 261

typographic image, 201

Museum of Fine Arts (Boston), sign,
233–35

Museum of Modern Art (NYC),
poster, 264

Museum of the USS Constitution,
exhibit, 282–83

N

National Bickford/Foremost, symbol, 191

National Gallery of Art and the
Museum of Art, Rhode Island
School of Design, catalogue
cover and poster, 248–49

National Museum of American Art,
Smithsonian Institution, double
page spread, 252

NEPTCO (New England Printed
Tape), symbol, 196

Nesting boxes exercise, 126–27

Nevelson, Louise, 15

Non-reptitive identity program,
218–19

O

Oakwood Comprehensive Training
Center, environmental design,
222–25

One of a kind, 260

P

Photogram, 100

Photography books, design, 268–69

Posters, 186–89

balance in, 26, 242–47

Brown University, 231

Dartmouth College, 220–21, 232

Department of Architecture,
Rhode Island School of Design,
188–89

Earth Zero, 258–59

for exhibitions, 242–44, 246, 262

Light Gallery, 253

Museum of Art, Rhode Island
School of Design, 248–49

Museum of Modern Art (NYC), 264

Solomon R. Guggenheim Museum,
186–87, 242–44, 245

Presbyterian Church (USA), seal and
symbol, 212–15

Professional practice, 176–295

design as a business, 181

design commissions, 183–285

from school to studio, 178

from student to professional, 179

Proposals:

clients, 290

submitting, 183

Providence Art Club, announcement,
230

R

Repetitive identity programs, 218

Rhode Island School of Design,
(RISD), 9, 12

catalogue cover and poster, 248–49

catalogue covers, 254, 261

Roger Williams College (architecture division):
　brochure cover, 258
　signs, 240–41
Roger Williams Foods, symbol, 205
Roitman & Son, Inc., identification sign, 238
Rot, Diter, 261

S

Sapphire Bay, symbol, 204
Save the Bay, symbols/signs, 168
Scale relationship, 230–31
Scientific American Library, series design, 274–75
Sequencing, relating, and pacing, 266–73
　book design, 266–67, 268
Serif typefaces, sans serif typeface compared to, 27
Shortline, Inc., symbol, 198–99
Signs, 233–41
　Big Canoe, 239
　Boston City Hospital, 202–3
　dual visual meaning, 202–3
　Foremost Lithograph, 236–37
　Museum of Fine Arts (Boston), 233–35
　Roger Williams College (architecture division), 240–41
　Roitman & Son, Inc., 238
　without words, 222–25
Simpson, Francis and Virgil, anniversary poster, 247
Siskind, Aaron, 15, 20, 156–61, 270
Solar Cities and Towns, symbol, 204
Solomon R. Guggenheim Museum:
　catalogue, 266–67
　catalogue cover, 265
　exhibition posters, 242–44
　performance posters, 245
　poster, 186–87
　visual identity, 218–19

Sonesta International Hotels, symbol, 97
Specifications, typesetting, 143
Student assignments:
　form and structure, 66–87
　letterform studies, 20–65
　maple leaf exercise, 18–19
　overview exercise, 86–87
　ten-step sequences, 88–140
Sun in symbols, 204–5
Symbols, 164–69, 184–85
　Audobon Society of Rhode Island, 164–67
　Banco de Edwards, 200
　Bay State Abrasives, 195
　Brier Manufacturing, 192
　Brown University, 194
　Cannon Design, 208
　Color Concentrate Corporation, 184
　Community Preparatory School, 210
　constantly moving Symbols, 209
　International Institute of Rhode Island, 169
　Manomet Observatory, 185
　Merrimack Valley Textile Museum, 206
　Metropolitan Opera, 209
　Morris Museum of Arts and Sciences, 211
　Mount Holyoke College, 184
　National Bickford/Foremost, 191
　NEPTCO (New England Printed Tape), 196
　Presbyterian Church (USA), 212–15
　Roger Williams Food, 205
　Sapphire Bay, 204
　Save the Bay, 168
　Shortline, Inc., 198–99
　Solar Cities and Towns, 204
　Sonesta International Hotels, 97
　sun in symbols, 204–5
　Tools for Training, 169
　Twins Foundation, 193

T

Ten-step sequences, 88–140
　containers/contents, 134–35
　essence of an object, 128–33
　form, analyzing, 124–25
　handtool, function of, 96–64
　letters, transformation of, 106–9
　steps, sequence, and series, 88–95
　3/D form with ten expandable/ retractable parts, design of, 126–27
　type/image, 136–40
　variations on a theme, 123
　visual comparisons, 113–22
　visual stories, combining, 104–5
　words, visualization of, 110–12
3/D structure, 282–83
Thumbtack exercise, 124–25
Time, space, and position, 228–29
Tools for Training, symbols/signs, 16
Townley, Hugh, 224
Trinity Repertory Theatre, time, space, and position, 228–29
Tufts University School of Medicine, street marker, 284–85
Twins Foundation, symbol, 193
Typefaces:
　personalities of, 27
　selecting, 141
Type/image, 136–40
Typesetting, 143
Typography:
　design application, 172–75
　Fireworks (Jennings) assignment, 148–49
　graphic standards manual, 171
　Harlem Document (Siskind) assignment, 156–61
　hierarchy of information assignment, 154–55
　Invisible Cities (Calvino) assignment, 152–53
　and letterforms, 140–77

greetings from outerspace
    assignment, 150–51, 163
symbols/signs, 164–69
typographic form, 143–64

U
Udvardy, John, 232
Union College, announcement, 260
University of Rhode Island, double-
    page spread, 250–51

V
Visual comparisions, 113–22
Visual connections/relationships, 82–85
Visual noise, 12–13
Visual switch, 194–96
Visual sympathy, 262–65
Void (1957), 16

W
Walk-through exhibit, Mayo Clinic, 281
Weston, Brett, 270
Words, visualization of, 110–12
Worth Publishers, college textbook
    design, 270–73